P9-DHD-855

A MENTOR'S PERSPECTIVE
ON REIGNITING SUCCESS

Tuesday Morning
Coaching

Eight Simple Truths

to Boost Your Career

and Your Life

Medical Library
North Memorial Health Care
3300 Oakdale Avenue North
Robbinsdale, MN 55422

David Cottrell

Author of the *Monday Morning* series

Tuesday Morning
Coaching

Eight Simple Truths to Boost Your Career and Your Life

Copyright © 2010 CornerStone Leadership Institute. All rights reserved.

No part of this book may be reproduced in any form without written permission in advance from the publisher. International rights and foreign translations available only through negotiation with CornerStone Leadership Institute.

The companies and events portrayed in this book are fictitious. Any resemblance to actual people, names, companies, and events is purely coincidental.

Inquiries regarding permission for use of the material contained in this book should be addressed to:

CornerStone Leadership Institute
P.O. Box 764087
Dallas, TX 75376
888.789.LEAD

Printed in the United States of America
ISBN: 978-0-9819242-5-0

Credits

Editors	Alice Adams, Austin, TX
	Juli Baldwin, The Baldwin Group, Dallas, TX
	info@BaldwinGrp.com
Copy editor	Kathleen Green, Positively Proofed, Plano, TX
	info@positivelyproofed.com
Design, art direction, and production	Melissa Monogue, Back Porch Creative, Plano, TX
	info@backporchcreative.com

Table of Contents

"All great truths are simple in final analysis,
and easily understood;
if they are not, they are not great truths."

NAPOLEON HILL

Foreword

When Ryan Harris asked me to be his mentor and then later to write the foreword to this book, I was deeply honored. To be a mentor and coach is humbling and exciting.

I was fortunate to have a wonderful experience with a mentor many years ago who helped shape my life. At that point in time, my career was at a crossroads. I had been a successful leader for many years, but then things changed. Life and work became a real struggle, and I had to do something to get back on track. Not only had I become negative and cynical, but I also was having a hard time believing anybody really cared about me or my problems. At that low point in my life, I was a long way from being the kind of person I wanted to be.

I needed counsel and advice from someone I respected who would listen and offer suggestions without judging me. I decided to call Tony Pearce, one of my father's friends and a successful business leader. In his semi-retirement, he devoted most of his time to writing books and coaching top executives.

Tony was exactly the type of person I aspired to be …
successful, authentic, wise, respected, confident and caring.
Thankfully, Tony agreed to mentor me, and that is when my
life changed. Through his coaching, I was able to get my
career – and my life – back on track. Today, I am a consultant
to organizations around the globe. In almost every consulting
role, I pass on many of the lessons Tony shared with me.
I also shared my learning from my Mondays with Tony in
a book, *Monday Morning Mentoring: Ten Lessons to Guide You Up
the Ladder.*

You see, one of Tony's stipulations for mentoring me was that
when we completed our time together, I would commit to
teach others what I had learned. So when Ryan Harris, a
former associate, contacted me not too long ago to seek my
advice, I sensed yet another opportunity to "pass it on."

In hindsight, the call from Ryan was eerily similar to the one
I made to Tony Pearce. I remembered Ryan as an energetic,
dynamic, positive and smart young man in our organization.
He began his career in our manager trainee program and was
clearly on the fast track. He was a quick-study and confident. In
team meetings, he stood out, mainly because he could easily
think outside thebox. But he was equally strong in his analysis
of new processes and in his ability to tweak solutions to
perfectly fit emerging problems and issues.

Yet the man who called me was not the confident, self-assured
Ryan Harris I had known. Instead, he sounded frustrated,
overwhelmed and beaten down by business and by life. After
describing his situation, Ryan said he needed to "reboot"
himself and get back on track so he could move forward. It

appeared that both success and happiness were eluding him, and I could sense that he was definitely burned out.

I told Ryan that I would work with him if he would commit to two things – not coincidentally, the same two things Tony asked me to commit to.

I explained to Ryan that we would follow a structured process that would require us to spend significant time together. I would commit my time to him if he would commit to meeting for one hour each Tuesday morning for eight weeks at my home.

When Tony mentored me, I had to commit to 10 meetings, but our sessions were on Monday mornings. Due to my schedule, Ryan and I met on Tuesdays rather than Mondays. Actually, there was something I liked about meeting on Tuesdays. Like Ryan and myself, many people achieve success early in their career, on "Monday" so to speak. But often, through the twists and turns of business and life, we get down the road a bit and discover we've gotten off track. Tuesdays are for getting back on track and taking our lives to the next level.

The second requirement was the more important one to me, just as it had been to Tony, and that was that Ryan must commit to teach others what he learned. It's been said that there are three parts to leadership – Learn It, Live It and Share it. The "Share It" stage is the most rewarding of all because when you share what you've learned, you give back and contribute to others' success.

I was pleased when Ryan readily committed. I was also pleased because I suspected that I would get at least as much out of our meetings as he would … and I was right.

Ryan showed up on time to every one of our Tuesday morning meetings, ready to work. And, man, did he deliver on his commitment to share what he learned! You hold the result of that commitment in your hands.

Enjoy the journey, apply what you learn and then … pass it on!

Jeff Walters
Coach to Ryan Harris

Prologue

Eighteen months ago …

Things were not going well. I was in a severe and prolonged personal and professional slump. Business had been tough for quite awhile, and every time I thought things were about to get better, a new problem would rear its ugly head.

I was frustrated, angry, and embarrassed. After months of trying to work myself out of my problems, I finally came to the realization that I needed to seek advice. As arrogant as it may sound, I had never needed counsel from anyone until then.

So I reached out to Jeff Walters, hoping he could coach me and help me revive my career. I had worked on Jeff's team at a large organization for several years. He was a fantastic leader, and I'd always admired the way he handled success as well as the challenges our organization faced. Even though he probably was not aware of the positive influence he had on me, he was a role model. I was amazed at how he could take a complex issue and simplify it so that everyone could understand what needed to be done.

I had heard that Jeff had become a very successful consultant and author after he left the company. I'd even read one of his books, *Monday Morning Mentoring*, and found it to be a huge help with some difficult issues I was facing with my team. In fact, it was in referring back to his book one day that I had the idea to contact him. I remembered that when he was with our organization, he had frequently talked about "the simple truths of success." He had been a great coach and mentor to the people on our team. I wondered if he would be willing to coach me now, even though we don't work together anymore.

I was doubtful. Jeff was now a big-time consultant, working with major corporations. How could he possibly have time for individuals like me?

But I figured I had nothing to lose. I was at the point where I was willing to explore every option. So I tracked Jeff down and called him. When I explained my situation and told him I was willing to do whatever was necessary to get myself out of my slump, he graciously offered to mentor me. There was a catch, however. Jeff explained he would coach me only if I agreed, in turn, to coach others – to teach others the lessons he would share with me.

Immensely grateful, I accepted his offer. But I have to admit I was a little skeptical. I mean, my issues were personal as well as business related. I was certain he could help me with my career, but I wasn't so sure he would be able to help me improve my personal life. I quickly discovered I didn't need to worry. The positive impact of my Tuesday morning coaching sessions with Jeff on both my career and my personal life were dramatic.

You will learn from reading this book, just as I learned from Jeff, that success is not a secret. It's also not doing just one thing better than most people. No, success is created – and sustained – by discovering simple truths from many people and then applying them to your unique situation.

I am honored you are investing your time in reading *Tuesday Morning Coaching* and ask you, in turn, to teach others the wisdom that Jeff shared with me.

The First Tuesday

No Matter What!

It was a beautiful morning when I drove to Jeff's home for our first meeting. He had moved out of the city to a pristine lakefront community, and the 45-minute drive gave me time to think. But that wasn't necessarily a good thing. The thought that these meetings with Jeff might be a waste of time haunted me. *Of course*, I reasoned, if things were great, *I would have never called Jeff in the first place.* The truth was, something had to change.

As I pulled into Jeff's driveway, I could not help but notice the freshness and perfection of his property. The house itself was not huge, but everything outside his home was immaculate. The smell of blooming flowers drifted on the breeze off the lake. The walkway leading up to the spacious porch perfectly matched the pavers of the driveway. The grass, still sparkling with the last of the morning dew, provided a crisp contrast to the well-tended and manicured shrubbery. Jeff's place mirrored the way he used to run our organization – everything was in its proper place.

I had arrived about 10 minutes before our scheduled 7:00 a.m. meeting time. I remembered from my days working with Jeff that he was a stickler for starting and ending any meeting on time, so there was no way I was going to be late for my coaching sessions with him.

"Hello, Ryan!" Jeff said, meeting me at the door and extending his hand. "I'm honored you called and asked to come see me. It's been awhile since we've seen each other. You look terrific!"

Look terrific? I thought to myself. I felt like I'd been beaten up physically and emotionally for months.

Jeff invited me in and then laid down the book he was carrying on a nearby table. When he asked if I'd like a quick tour of his home, I enthusiastically accepted. The home also reflected Jeff's personality. The hardwood floors and classic furniture looked like they should be featured in an interior decorating magazine. Everything was first class.

When we reached the library, an incredible room filled with books and memorabilia, I immediately noticed he had set aside several pictures of our team from the time we had worked together. The pictures reflected good times … really good times. We couldn't help but smile, laugh and reminisce about the good ol' days. It had been a long time since I'd experienced the feeling of success. It was good to remember how it felt.

As I followed Jeff into the kitchen, I was reminded of some of the characteristics that I had always admired in him – his positive attitude, striking confidence and zest for life. As he poured a cup of coffee for each of us, I asked about his wife. "Is Susan around? I'd hoped to say 'hi' while I was here."

"Unfortunately, she's not," Jeff said. "She goes to one of those early morning boot camp workouts at the gym every Tuesday and Thursday. But she did want me to tell you 'hello' and that she's sorry she'll miss you."

After a few more minutes of catching up about our families, he looked at his watch and said it was time to get down to business. "It's a gorgeous morning. Let's sit out on the deck. Is that okay with you?"

"Sure," I said as we each grabbed our coffee cups and he led the way outside.

Jeff's home sat on a small bluff directly above the shore of the lake. Spanning the entire length of the back of the house was a covered deck artfully arranged with outdoor furniture and planters filled with flowers and ferns. My guess was that Jeff often held meetings out here on the deck. And why wouldn't he? The view was spectacular.

"I appreciate you reaching out to me, Ryan," Jeff said as we settled into two cushioned chairs. "Seeking an outsider's advice is a good and courageous move. I could tell from your phone call that you needed someone to help you sort through your issues, and I'm honored you chose me.

"I believe I'll be able to help because I've been right where you are. In fact, a few years ago, I reached out to a friend – Tony Pearce – who helped me work my way out of a leadership slump. Everyone needs a coach occasionally … someone who can provide new perspective on issues that may seem overwhelming.

"I like the term that you used on the phone to describe your situation," Jeff continued. "Do you remember what you said?"

"Sure I do. I told you I needed to reboot my life and career, just like I have to reboot my computer occasionally when it gets cluttered and slows down. But right now, I'm burned out and, quite frankly, tired of working hard but going nowhere. The reason I'm here is because I'm ready to move forward."

Jeff took a sip of coffee and sat silently for a moment, staring out over the lake. Finally he said, "Everyone gets burned out occasionally. Burnout is created by stress – a constant level of stress, in some cases. When this happens, it can be devastating to your job performance but, more importantly, it can destroy your physical health at the same time.

"When you're burned out, the first thing you need to figure out is if the situation is a long-term challenge or merely a short-term inconvenience. From what you've told me, you are well beyond the short-term inconvenience stage. Am I right?"

"No doubt. I'm definitely on the long-term side," I answered. "In fact, this has been going on quite a while. I've tried to address the situation on my own … I just haven't had much success."

"If it's not a short-term inconvenience, then you need to talk to someone about it ... and I'm glad you called me," Jeff reassured. "Holding the stress inside only creates more stress. By sharing with someone you trust, you will discover that there are things you can do to improve the situation.

"One of the keys to getting back on track is to not overreact. You see, when you're in burnout mode, everything is exaggerated. If you're in a rut – and this is where you are right now – you need to stop digging and making the rut deeper. In times of stress and/or ambiguity, you should never make long-term, life-changing decisions. However, this also is not the time to just sit there and hope things improve. Never, in the history of mankind, has any situation improved on its own while people sat there doing nothing."

"I understand," I said. "That's why I'm here."

Jeff reached for a small notebook that was on the table between us. "Before we get started, I think we need to set some ground rules so we can make the best use of our time together. With that in mind, I took the liberty of drawing these up. Tell me what you think."

He pushed the spiral-bound notebook titled "Tuesday Morning Lessons" across the table to me. As I opened it, I saw where he had listed four simple rules on the first page:

Ground Rules for Tuesday Morning Lessons:

1. Commit to be on time and ready to work at 7:00 a.m. for eight consecutive weeks.

2. Complete the "homework assignments."

3. Tell the truth.

4. Try something different.

As I read through the rules, Jeff offered, "Let me go over each of these so we completely understand our commitment. First, we need to honor each other's time by being prompt and consistent in our meetings. Second, I will ask you to do some 'homework assignments.' These will usually involve you meeting with people who are outside of your normal sphere of colleagues and peers. Completing these assignments will be crucial if you're going to reignite your life.

"Third," he continued, "one of the most important aspects of this process is for you to discover the truth. It's also one of the most difficult. But very little that is worthwhile comes easily. In fact, 'difficult' almost always comes before 'easy.' Most people focus on what they want the truth to be … in our sessions, we will focus on the truth as it is.

"Socrates once said, 'Knowing thyself is the height of wisdom.' It appears to me that you may not have been completely honest with yourself." Jeff paused to let that sink in. Then he continued, "If you'd been honest with yourself, you likely would have come for help a long time ago. It's never a good idea to lie to yourself, no matter how painful the truth may be.

"Fourth," he concluded, "at the end of each session, I will ask you to try something different going forward. If you are serious about changing your situation, you have to do things differently. After all, what you've been doing is what got you into the mess you're in now. Nothing changes if nothing changes. If you're not willing to think and act differently, we're wasting each other's time."

The ground rules seemed clear and simple enough. I was a little uneasy about what he might ask me to do differently, but I was so tired of being in my mess that I was game for anything. I looked at Jeff. "I can do these. I'm ready to get going."

"Great," said Jeff, settling back in his chair. "The reason I gave you a spiral-bound notebook is so you would have a place to keep all your notes. You'll especially need it when you do your homework assignments … using a laptop or PDA won't be practical, and people tend to misplace loose papers. You can always type up your notes later if you wish. Plus, many people believe that handwriting rather than typing allows us to tap into the right side of our brains where creativity, conceptual thinking and problem solving exist. So take good notes in there," he concluded. "It may be something you want to pass on to your kids someday.

"So let's begin with you bringing me up to speed about what's been going on in your life that made you want to connect with me."

For the better part of the next hour, I did all the talking. Jeff listened without saying much, other than asking an occasional question.

I described the issues I was facing. "When you and I worked together, I was at the top of my game, or at least I thought I was. I felt I had earned my success, and no one could take it away from me. Little did I know the economy was going to go south, and the things that had worked in the past wouldn't work anymore. I've noticed that everything in my life is connected. My frustrations and unhappiness at work have seeped into other areas of my life. When things aren't going well at work, that affects my health and my home life. And my health and home life impact how well I do my job. And because of the complexity of these connections, I haven't been able to get myself back on the right track. I don't seem to have enough time for my family or my job, and things – important things – are slipping by without me even noticing.

"In the early stages of my career, success came relatively easy. For whatever reason, now everything has become more difficult. Honestly, I feel like my mojo is gone, and I hope you can help me get it back. You always seemed to prosper during the rollercoaster ups and downs of business as well as life in general. You were an inspiration to me. No matter what was happening, you always had it together."

When I had finally finished, Jeff started talking. "First, I want you to know that the problems you're facing are not unique to you. Even though we tend to think our challenges are rare and unique, they aren't. Everyone faces similar issues. In fact, I've been exactly where you are – facing the same problems, the same frustrations – and many others have been there as well. Even the most successful people have these challenges.

"Are you familiar with Steve Jobs of Apple?" he asked.

"Sure!" I responded. "The products his organization has developed and produced over the years have literally changed the way the world communicates. The man is brilliant."

"You're absolutely right. He is brilliant," Jeff affirmed. "Steve was 20 years old when he began Apple in his parents' garage. Before his 30th birthday, he'd built the company into a $2 billion empire. However, even with his past successes, the board of directors wanted to change things. So they fired him … and remember, he was only 30 years old."

"Steve Jobs … fired from Apple? I didn't know that."

"Yes. He was fired from the company he created. Most people would be bitter and hurt – and I'm sure Steve probably felt those same emotions – but he decided to look at his new situation as a freedom rather than an insult. Later, he said getting fired from Apple was the best thing that ever happened to him because it allowed him the freedom to be creative again.

"Jobs went on to begin another company – NeXT, a software company – and then bought Pixar in 1986. Pixar is the animated movie company that created *Finding Nemo* and *Toy Story*, among others. And guess who bought NeXT?"

"Apple?" I asked.

"That's right! Kind of ironic, isn't it? And the rest, as they say, is history. Today, Steve Jobs is once again at the helm of Apple.

He says his success in business and his strong relationship with his family came as a result of his termination from Apple.

"So there's no reason to be embarrassed or to dwell on where you are, Ryan. That just wastes time and energy. What you are currently experiencing is the same thing that happens to many others. People get caught up during life's journey and forget to take care of the basics. They lose sight of what they are trying to accomplish. Things are moving along smoothly, and the smoother it is, the easier it is to become distracted. They tend to lose focus. Then when a crisis comes along, they overreact and search for somewhere to put the blame instead of moving forward.

"Your situation, like Steve Jobs getting fired, could be a blessing. Many times you learn best when you're in the middle of a storm – right where you are now. No matter how bleak the situation, if you think about it, you'll realize that there is always something that can be done, and there is always something that you can do. In this situation, what you can do is develop a plan to improve your situation, and that is where we need to spend our time and energy.

"Second, it's not too late to change," Jeff continued. "Based on my own experience, I assure you that now is the best time for you to change. You still have a great life ahead of you. You just need to work your way out of the rut you're in. Few people have the courage to take the step you've already taken – to reach out for some guidance and coaching. That first step is the toughest, so you're already making progress. You begin growing when you accept the truth about your situation."

"So what do we do from here?" I asked, somewhat impatiently. "I'm ready to do what needs to be done."

"Okay," Jeff shot back. "Do you remember when we worked together, I often talked with our team about 'the simple truths of success'?"

"I definitely remember you telling us about them, but I have to admit that I can't recall the truths themselves," I answered somewhat sheepishly.

"The principles I talked to you about years ago haven't changed, and they will be the same long after we are gone," Jeff explained. "Over the next eight weeks, we'll revisit those simple truths and learn more about them so you can get back on the path to success.

"By the way," he said, "why do you think I asked you to meet with me for eight weeks?"

I thought for a minute. "Is it because there are eight truths to cover?" Secretly, I didn't want that to be the right answer because I'd been hoping it wouldn't take all eight weeks to sort through my issues and develop a plan.

"Well, you're right ... at least partially. We'll talk about eight truths. But the reason I suggested eight weeks is because, during that period of time, a lot of things will happen in your life that will attempt to throw you and our meetings off course. During the next eight weeks, we'll have a chance to see some of life's curveballs thrown your way – and probably my way as well – and we'll take a crack at them as they come.

"Also, it will take us all eight weeks because I've found that long-term success is not the result of one defining change. Rarely does that happen," Jeff said as he leaned toward me to emphasize his point. "Success comes from developing the habit of doing several small – even simple – actions. Each of those actions are independent yet connected ... sort of like a tree branch. All of the leaves are independent, but they are connected by a strong and sturdy stem. The simple truths are the leaves, and you are the stem."

"So, in other words, I should count on all eight weeks," I said, trying to hide my disappointment.

"That's right ... eight weeks. We cannot shortchange the process. Ultimately, it will pay dividends for you and me. I'm confident of that."

Jeff then shifted gears. "By the way, I love to read to my grandchildren. Every time I read a children's book, I'm amazed at what I learn. Yesterday I was reading one of Aesop's Fables to Noah, my 3-year-old grandson. You may think those fables are old and worn, but the wisdom is still applicable today.

"Do you remember the fable about the Tortoise and the Hare?"

"Sure," I replied. "It's been a while, but what I remember is that the Tortoise won the race."

"Well, I'm glad you remember the bottom line. But what you need to pay attention to is what happened to the Hare. To refresh your memory, the Hare ridiculed the Tortoise ... said he had short little feet and was as slow as molasses. He told the Tortoise he was 'so slow that sheep count you before they go to sleep.'

"The Tortoise laughed at the Hare and said that even though the Hare was as swift as the wind, he would beat the Hare in a race. 'Impossible!' said the Hare, and the bet was on.

"The fox started the big race, and off they went. The Tortoise never for a moment stopped. But the confident, cocky Hare stopped to rest. After waking up from his nap, he ran toward the finish line and saw that the Tortoise had already won and was comfortably dozing after his victory.

"Do you remember the moral of the story?" Jeff asked.

"It was something like 'perseverance beats speed,'" I responded.

"Yes, that is one of the morals. What if the Hare had run straight to the finish line? Who would have won?"

"The Hare, of course," I answered.

"Then perseverance would not have beaten speed." Jeff was getting wound up. "You see, the problem with the Hare was that he was so consumed with his talent that he forgot to use it. He became distracted by the comfort of taking a nap. The Tortoise had perseverance but he also was not distracted – he was focused on the finish line.

"I've found that successful people are not distracted by their success. They are focused on mastering a combination of several simple truths that – put together – create ongoing success.

"The first truth I want to introduce to you today is about mastering the attitude of 'No Matter What.' No Matter What means that, regardless of what is going on around us, we have to accept responsibility and move forward. You see, every person is ultimately responsible for who they become and what they accomplish in life. It's up to you to take control.

"Along life's journey, people and circumstances will distract you and, if you allow them to, prevent you from moving forward. You may be distracted by people who are threatened by your success and don't want you to succeed. Sometimes, other situations seem more important. There are plenty of distractions if you pay attention to them. But no great accomplishments will happen if you allow yourself to be continually distracted by your surroundings.

"Why people are surprised when distractions and obstacles pop up baffles me," Jeff continued. "There is no reason to be surprised ... you can count on them showing up. It's going to happen. Once an obstacle emerges, that's when you have to make the decision to retreat or move forward, and this is where you are right now. It's decision-making time. Do you retreat or pay the price to move forward – No Matter What?"

"I'm ready to move forward ... definitely!" I said. "But how do I do that? Do you believe that if I just hang in there through thick and thin – or No Matter What – things will ultimately work out? What if the situation I'm facing is unrealistic or unachievable?"

"Certainly, it has to pass the 'reasonable test,'" Jeff pointed out. "But most of the time people quit because the task gets tough, not because the task is unreasonable.

"The No Matter What attitude doesn't even kick in until you are well into the tough stage," he explained. "When things get tough is when people tend to retreat and give up. Many times they quit right when success is just over the horizon because they are focused on the distractions rather than moving forward," he said, stopping to make sure I got the point. "And, Ryan, success is only achieved through repeated introspection and moving forward, despite failures along the way.

"Don't get me wrong," Jeff continued. "Having a No Matter What mentality does not guarantee success. It is just one of several factors that help create success. However, a No Matter What mentality will remind you to consider alternatives that may not be obvious at first glance."

"I'm not sure I follow that last part," I interrupted.

"Let me explain it this way," Jeff said. "One of the greatest lessons I've learned is that keeping an open mind to different alternatives will expose opportunities that you did not even know existed. Assuming that there is only one or two ways to solve a problem can be the root of failure. When you only focus on one way to do something, you limit yourself. I've never seen a challenge for which multiple alternatives were not available. But most people don't look for those alternatives because they may not be readily apparent. Remember what we said earlier – people tend to give up when things get tough.

"Having a No Matter What perspective forces you to explore all options, providing you with an opportunity for success. People who quit or spend their time looking for excuses, well, they can just say 'goodbye' to that opportunity.

"Here is how you can put a No Matter What attitude into action. Try this exercise the next time you're faced with a situation where you feel stuck," Jeff suggested. "Write down the numbers 1 through 10 on a sheet of paper. Then start looking for at least 10 alternatives to your situation. Force yourself to think outside of the box. Consider possibilities that might seem 'out there.' Many times you will discover that the best solution is the 10th one you wrote down – the one you had to rack your brain to come up with."

After jotting down the description of that exercise in my notebook, I looked up. "I like that. I'm already thinking of a few situations where I can use that."

"Great," Jeff responded as he checked his watch for the time. "Before we wrap up for this week, I want to share a powerful piece of advice that my mentor, Tony Pearce, shared with me regarding career development." Jeff smiled as he thought back to his own mentoring experience.

"Tony told me that when it came to my career development, I had to understand the difference between being the driver and being a passenger. He used the analogy of driving a car as opposed to merely being a passenger in the car. You see, passengers are free to look around, to be distracted," Jeff explained. "As a driver, you must focus on the road, not on distractions. Drivers – at least safe drivers – can't be distracted by text messages, phone calls or eating, whereas a passenger can be. If you're in the driver's seat – and that's where you want to be when it comes to your career – you have to keep your focus on the road, No Matter What.

"You have power over where you focus ... that is a choice you make. You can choose to focus on improving things, or you can choose to look for other people or situations to blame," Jeff said in a stern and serious way.

"A few minutes ago, you mentioned that the economy was to blame for you being in the position you are now. But in truth, that's probably an exaggeration. The economy has been tough, no doubt about it. However, the economy does not have power over where you focus. The economy doesn't dictate your next move. You control those choices.

"Look around. You'll see successful people in every economy. Those people are the ones who have discovered that success is ultimately realized by making more good choices than bad choices ... and recovering quickly when they do make a bad choice. These people know their choices provide their next direction, toward or away from what they are trying to achieve. Regardless of economic conditions, your personal and professional success depends on repeating good choices ... and not repeating bad choices," Jeff emphasized.

"If you watch closely, you also will see that successful people make choices others don't like to make. They may not like making difficult choices. Who does? But they realize there is often a greater purpose in choosing to do some things they may not want to do," he said. "Success is not about luck or the economy. It's about making a conscious choice that No Matter What, you will keep moving forward toward your goals."

Jeff took his last sip of coffee. "Ryan, our time is about up for today. I learned a lot about you, and I look forward to learning more. I'm excited about your future. Thanks for asking for my help."

"Thank *you*," I jumped in, "for taking time out of your busy schedule to coach me. I truly appreciate it."

"You're welcome," he responded. "Now, let's talk about your first homework assignment. As I mentioned earlier, during the next eight weeks, we – both you and I – will be learning from several people who are successful in fields different than yours."

"Excuse me for interrupting," I interjected, "but how will that help me if they are in different professions?"

Jeff smiled. "Good question. Success is not profession-specific. The simple truths of success are constant across all fields and professions. The people you're going to meet consistently exhibit positive traits that would allow them to be successful in any field."

"Okay," I said. "But why did you say we were going to learn from them?"

"Because I'm quite certain that I, too, will learn something new when you report back about your meetings with them. I call it 'circular coaching,'" Jeff answered. "And, by the way, that's one of the beautiful things about mentoring – the coach often learns just as much as the person being coached.

"So ... your homework. Before our meeting next week, I want you to arrange a meeting with the top salesperson in your organization and ask that guy or gal why their results are better than the average salesperson in the organization.

Write your findings in your notebook, and let's begin our discussion next week with what you learned from that meeting."

Jeff stood and, as he walked me through the house to the front door, he asked, "So, is there anything you will do this week to make your situation better?"

"Well, what you said about having a No Matter What attitude makes sense. But there are so many external factors that get in my way," I said, almost apologetically. "But what I can do is be more aware of distractions, try to make better choices and see how it goes. I'm also going to promise that I will stop being surprised by distractions that come my way."

"Write those things in the notebook," Jeff suggested as we walked out on the porch. "When you write things down, it clarifies and reinforces your commitment to doing them. If you simply tell me what you want to do, there is really no commitment to getting it done.

"Also, read this when you get to your office," Jeff said as he handed me a sealed note card.

I thanked him again for his time and told him I was already looking forward to next Tuesday.

As I drove back into the city, I felt frustrated with myself and with the process of having to work myself out of my rut. Had I allowed the distractions of success to keep me from maintaining that success? Did Jeff's No Matter What philosophy really work? Would these sessions make a difference? Even though I had plenty of questions, I had promised both Jeff and myself I would try something different and see what would happen.

When I arrived at my office, I opened the envelope from Jeff. On the front of the note card was a picture of a tree in the middle of a frozen lake. Ice was creeping up the tree's trunk. In the background, the sun was rising. The caption below the picture said: "Press on. Your defining moment may arrive just when you feel surrounded by adversity."

Pretty appropriate, I thought. *I definitely feel surrounded by adversity.*

Inside the card was a handwritten note from Jeff:

Ryan,

Congratulations for having the courage to seek advice. This step alone indicates to me that you are willing to discover the simple truths of success.

The picture on the front of this card may visually describe where you are right now. Just remember to press on – No Matter What. And remember, Ryan, that you're not alone. We're going to take this leg of your journey together.

Thank you for allowing me to share my experiences with you.

See you next Tuesday.
Jeff

As I read the note, I felt confident I had gone to the right person for advice. Jeff was on my side and wanted to help me. Maybe change for the better was on the horizon.

I wrote in my notebook:

No Matter What

Key Points:

✔ My problems are not unique to me, so there is no reason to be embarrassed or to dwell on where I am.

✔ Long-term success is not the result of one defining change. It comes from developing the habit of embracing several small, simple truths of success.

✔ I begin growing when I accept the truth about my situation.

✔ No Matter What means that regardless of what is going on around me, I will accept responsibility and take control. There is always something that can be done and something that I can do.

✔ I have power over where I focus ... that is a choice I make.

✔ I am in the driver's seat when it comes to my career and my life.

My Assignment: Learn success truths from the top salesperson in our company.

Do Something Different:

1. Use the No Matter What exercise to explore all options when the journey gets tough.

2. Focus on moving forward rather than on the distractions.

3. Press on ... my defining moment may arrive just when I feel surrounded by adversity.

The Second Tuesday

... And Then Some

I drove into Jeff's driveway at exactly 6:45 a.m. As I parked the car, I noted he was watering the plants in his flowerbed and listening to music or something through his earbuds.

"What music are you listening to?" I inquired.

"Actually, I'm not listening to music," Jeff smiled, removing the buds from his ears. "I'm listening to a local talk radio show. I listen to one particular show every day from 6:00 until 7:00. It's entertainment for me ... I usually get a few laughs because the people think they know a lot about everything, but they really don't know much about anything. Sometimes they get my blood boiling with their political rants. But, enough of their boola-boola," he said as he turned off the water and led me inside the house to the kitchen. "How was your week?"

"I actually had a pretty good week at work," I began. "We managed to avoid any major crises or distractions, but I kept in mind the No Matter What lesson you shared last week. In fact, I made a few No Matter What note cards and placed one next to my phone, on my desk and in my car. Almost everywhere I go, a No Matter What reminder is in sight."

"That's terrific," Jeff looked pleased as he poured our coffee. "Improvement begins when you accept responsibility ... No Matter What," Jeff said reassuringly. "And did you talk to one of your salespeople this week?"

"Yes. First thing last Thursday. I met with Kelley Baxley, and she was more than willing to share her success 'secrets' with me." I felt the cool breeze off the lake as we stepped out onto the deck.

"I bet she enjoyed talking with you," Jeff said, getting situated in his chair and motioning for me to sit in the one across the table from him. "Most successful people love to share their secrets. Thanks for taking the time to visit with her. Tell me, what did you learn?"

"Kelley is a legend in our organization," I began. "She's been our leading salesperson for many years. I'd never been in her office before, and I was amazed at the number of awards that were displayed there. It was pretty impressive. That's when I knew: If someone knows what it takes to be successful, Kelley would be that person. She has consistently been a top performer, regardless of the economy or which territory she was assigned. Our sales manager has moved her around quite a bit, and her results remain the same ... right at the top. And she told me that every time she returned from maternity leave, it wasn't long before she was right back at the top of our company's sales production rankings. She is doing something better than everyone else. That's what I wanted to learn.

"Aside from her stellar job performance, Kelley is also a superstar mom. She has three beautiful girls – 12, 7, and 5 years old – and is very involved in the kids' lives. I could tell that because she talked about her children more than she talked about her job. She also seemed to take pride in finding a balance between her life and her work.

"After we got to know each other, Kelley began explaining her sales process to me," I continued. She knew that I'm not a salesperson, but she wanted to make sure I understood the process. She explained the details of the sales cycle on a flip chart, and then asked me a simple question: 'What do you think the difference is between a good salesperson and a great salesperson?'

"I told her I honestly didn't know ... that's why I was meeting with her. But, remembering our conversation from last week, I said the great salesperson must have a better attitude and be willing to hang in there, No Matter What.

"You probably won't be surprised to hear that Kelley agreed that attitude and perseverance are two major factors for success. But she also pointed out that they are not the only factors. She said that people buy from those they enjoy being around and that a positive person is much more comfortable to be around than a negative, cynical person. Just as I was about to write down 'positive attitude' in my notebook, she said there are a lot of positive, persistent people on her sales team who are not great success stories."

"Well, you can't argue with that," Jeff said. "Remember we said last week that success comes from doing many things well. Having a positive, No Matter What mentality is just one of those things." He paused and then continued. "What did Kelley say she does differently from everyone else?"

"Interestingly," I said, "she said the main thing that she does differently than most is not something dramatic or major. She said she just does a little something extra every day, in every call and for every customer. Then she explained that most people stop when they have done what is required and that's when she is just getting started!

"For instance, she makes it a point to make one more sales call than is required every day – just one extra call every day. However, that one extra call adds up to 250 extra calls every year. She sells to 20 percent of those, so that gives her an extra 50 customers every year because of the one extra call every day. She refers to that extra call as the 'money call' because that's the one that separates her from her competitors who, by that point, have called it a day.

"In addition, she's developed an extensive database in which she enters every customer and prospect," I continued, referring to my notes. "Her database system sends her a daily reminder, prompting her with important facts about the customer – kids' names, birthdays, anniversaries, hobbies, interests, etc. – so she has an excuse to keep in contact with them. Kelley also writes at least one personal note to at least one customer every day. She said writing the note takes her about five minutes, but it is some of the best time that she can spend. She explained that her customers and prospects tend to remember those notes because they usually get e-mails rather than a personal, handwritten note that comes through the mail.

"Then she told me something pretty astounding," I said, leaning forward. "In more than five years, she has not lost a single customer to a competitor. She believes the reason is because she takes the extra steps to do something special every day to keep in touch."

"Kelley hasn't lost a customer in over five years?" Jeff questioned. "That is amazing. I wonder how many customers the average salesperson in your organization loses in a year."

"Well, I asked her that very question … and she said most tend to lose between 10 and 20 percent of their customers every year."

Jeff was obviously impressed with Kelley's record. "Wow! That is huge." He stopped and scribbled some calculations on his notepad. Then he looked up and announced, "Based on some quick math, over a 5-year period, she will have twice the number of customers as her peers if she continues at that pace. No wonder she's such a superstar!

"So, let me make sure I understand," he continued. "Kelley said the principal thing separating her from her peers and the competition is that she does a little something extra over and above what is required for all of her customers, right?"

"Right," I confirmed. "But she also acknowledged there are other factors that contribute to her success. Kelley said the number one factor for her success is having a process that allows her to go over and above for every customer."

Jeff was obviously pleased. "Ryan, thanks for meeting with Kelley. I'd heard about her success but didn't realize how incredible she actually is. She sounds like a special person who has figured out how to balance the important things, both at home and at work.

"Actually, Kelley is a great example of my second success truth – a principle I also try to practice every day. Kelley has what I call an 'And Then Some' mentality."

"And Then Some?" I repeated. "You mean she does what is expected ... and then some?"

"Exactly," Jeff said. "Kelley may not say it, but she has developed an And Then Some habit in everything she does. She provides 'lagniappe.' Have you ever heard that word?"

"No, can't say that I have," I said. "It sounds French, but that is as much as I know."

"Well," Jeff explained, "lagniappe is a French word that means 'a little something extra' or 'an unexpected gift.' That funny little word originated in French Creole mercantile stores in Louisiana many years ago. When a customer ordered 5 pounds of sugar, the clerk would dish out 5 pounds on the scale and then, with a smile, add an additional measure and say, 'Lagniappe!' That was the store owner's way of adding a little extra value and letting the customer know their business was important.

"Basically, those store owners were under-promising and over-delivering," Jeff went on. "Who knows? Maybe that extra measure was actually rolled into the price, but the customers' perception was that they were receiving a little something extra. Likewise, lagniappe is what Kelley delivers to her customers every day. She practices And Then Some every time she interacts with someone, giving them more than they expect."

Jeff excused himself and returned from the kitchen with the coffee pot. "Okay, here's a question for you, Ryan," he said, pouring more coffee into each cup. "Have you ever taken a taxi in New York City?"

I wondered where he was going with this out-of-the-blue question. "Sure, many times," I stammered. "Like everyone else, I've had some 'memorable' moments in New York City cabs. And I'm happy to say I survived them all ... although I wasn't so sure I'd survive at the time. So, I'm curious. Why do you ask?"

"Well, I know a cab driver in New York you should meet," Jeff replied, "and the experience you get when you hail Gerald Stokes' cab is definitely not a survival experience. Not by a long shot. In fact, it's an extraordinary experience.

"The first time I met Gerald was after I'd landed at LaGuardia. I was standing in line with everyone else – tired and hungry, ready to get to my hotel, and hoping to survive the cab ride. Much to my surprise, the cab that drove up for me was as clean as a whistle. The yellow paint on the car reflected like a mirror, it was so clean. Even the wheels were shiny. Then suddenly, out of the cab pops a middle-aged man, full of energy and enthusiasm.

"This guy – unlike any other cab driver I've encountered in my travels – was neatly dressed in black pants, starched white shirt and black tie. It wouldn't be an exaggeration to say he looked like a million bucks. And get this ... he was even smiling!" Jeff recalled. "He stretched out his hand and told me his name was Gerald and that it was a pleasure for him to drive me.

"While he was loading my luggage, he handed me a laminated mission statement. I keep it with me, because every time I go to New York, I call Gerald to pick me up." Jeff pulled a small card out of his wallet and handed it across the table to me. It read:

> **Gerald Stokes' Mission:**
> **Get you where you need to go –**
> **fast, comfortably, and safely.**
> **www.GeraldStokesCab.com**

"I thought the mission statement was interesting and creative," Jeff said after allowing me to copy the Web site address off the card and then he slipped it back into his wallet. "I don't know of any other cab drivers who have their own Web site or mission statement. When I got into the cab, I discovered that Gerald lived up to his mission. The car was spotless and that day's editions of the *New York Times* and *USA Today* were neatly folded, waiting for me. There was a thermos of hot coffee and another laminated card posted with the types of music and talk shows on the radio available during our ride.

"When Gerald got in the cab, he offered me some options for our ride. He said the fastest route at that time of day would take about 20 minutes. Or, if I would like to see some sites along the way, he would be glad to take me a different route. He also asked if I would prefer to listen to the radio or to be left to my own thoughts.

"Well, I was intrigued by this businessman and his approach," Jeff continued. "So I told him I'd prefer to skip the sightseeing and music. I wanted to talk to him on our way into Manhattan.

"Ryan, this guy was different from any other cabbie I'd ever ridden with," Jeff said. "As we were leaving the airport, I noticed he had yet another laminated card on his visor. It said, 'Gerald Stokes' Star Formula: Q+A=C.'

"Knowing me as you do, you can probably guess that I wasted no time asking him what the Gerald Stokes' Star Formula was all about ... and if he had always taken care of his customers like that. I mean, Gerald Stokes, a New York City cab driver, had made me feel like a million bucks!

"Gerald explained that he began his 'star treatment' three years ago. He also said you never know who the person in the back of your cab might be. So he made a commitment to treat every customer like a star. The formula he created was: the Quality of his service plus his Attitude toward the service he provides equals his Compensation, or Q+A=C."

Jeff seemed passionate about Gerald's commitment to quality service. "Then he told me that since he created and committed to the Gerald Stokes' Star Formula, his business had completely changed. Rarely did he have to wait for passengers in a cab line – I'd caught him in a rare gap between fares – most people called him for appointments. And here's the bottom line: since he began the Gerald Stokes' Star Treatment, his earnings had quadrupled!" Jeff stopped, but only to finish his now almost cool coffee before continuing his story.

"I asked Gerald why he used Gerald Stokes' Star Treatment rather than just Star Treatment, and he said that Gerald Stokes is more important than Star Treatment. He thought it was important for everyone to know his name, and this was just one additional way for them to remember," Jeff explained. "Then I asked him if other cabbies had broken the code and begun doing the same things he was doing. He said that nobody had, at least to his knowledge. 'They don't get it,' Gerald said. 'They've memorized all the reasons they can't do what I do and won't even try to separate themselves from the other cabbies.'"

"So let me see if I've got this right," I jumped in. "Gerald Stokes' Star Treatment is an And Then Some habit and the opposite of what most cabbies do, which is to try to get away with doing as little as they can."

"That's exactly right," Jeff said. "Other cabbies may be interested in being excellent, but most people are not committed enough to make excellence an everyday event. There is a big difference between being interested and being committed. For instance, have you noticed that when January 1st rolls around, everybody resolves to get into shape? In January, workout facilities are so crowded you have to stand in line for a machine. But come April, you can bring in your dogsled team and train them on the empty treadmills," he laughed. "The people you saw in January were mostly people who were interested. A few months later, only the committed remained.

"These committed individuals have just as many distractions and reasons to quit exercising as the people who vanished from the gym, but they made a commitment to keep going – No Matter What. The difference between mere interest and commitment are the habits you develop. It's those simple things that make the difference.

"Both Kelley and Gerald have said, in their own way, that going the extra mile isn't that much harder than doing what is required," Jeff pointed out. "Actually, it's often easier because there aren't many people traveling the extra mile ... so few, in fact, you may find yourself alone. But that is where real success happens.

"A key to success is developing and maintaining a habit of delivering 'And Then Some,'" Jeff concluded. "It doesn't matter if you call it 'going the extra mile,' 'star treatment,' or 'lagniappe.' What does matter, though, is that you live the simple guiding principle of And Then Some.

"And by the way," he added, "And Then Some doesn't just apply to people who work directly with customers like Kelley and Gerald. It applies to everyone – the person in the warehouse who retrieves the product and delivers it with a smile; the person in accounting who aggressively seeks alternatives to help the customer pay their bill; the CEO who takes the time to meet with all levels of employees monthly. Anyone can have an And Then Some mentality."

"It almost sounds too simple," I said after a few moments of silence. "But when I think about it, I learned the same principle from Mrs. Beck, my English Composition teacher in high school. I remember many times I'd turn in a paper, and she'd hand it back to me with a smile and say, 'You can do better than that.' Of course, I hated to hear those words, but she was always right. My original paper was usually pretty good, but after I'd go back and give it more, it was much better. If I'd just given And Then Some to begin with, it would have been much easier and faster – just like you said a minute ago. I'll also say that Mrs. Beck had more confidence in me than I had in myself ... and she obviously knew my work could be better."

Jeff agreed, "It's really simple, Ryan. Mrs. Beck wouldn't settle for just a passing grade from you. She wanted you to do what was expected ... And Then Some. When you do that, you stand out from the rest of the pack. Kelley, Gerald and you are living proof that the And Then Some principle works."

Changing subjects suddenly, Jeff asked, "How long has the receptionist at your office worked there?"

I rubbed my head as I thought. "I'm not sure. Julie has been there longer than I have," I finally answered. "I don't know her very well, but her personality and enthusiasm make a great impression on every person who comes into our building."

"Great!" Jeff said, clapping his hands at the same time. "Before our meeting next Tuesday, take Julie to lunch. I bet she has a wealth of information about what makes people successful. You may think it sounds odd to ask the receptionist what her perceptions are about successful people, but trust me on this. I think you'll be surprised."

Jeff paused, but only for a moment. "So, Ryan, what are you going to do differently this week, based on our conversation today?"

I looked at my notes and said, "Three things. First, I'm going to focus on being committed rather than simply interested. I think I've been like the others you talked about who live their lives looking for ways to get by doing less, and that needs to change.

"Second, I'm going to begin developing an And Then Some habit. Specifically, I think I'll make a list of the different ways in my life – both at work and at home – that I can go the extra mile or give some lagniappe.

"And finally, I'm making a commitment to myself to quit blaming others for my situation. When I left our meeting last week, I knew that No Matter What made sense, but I didn't know how hard it would be to develop a No Matter What habit. I found myself blaming people and justifying the same situations that put me into this rut in the first place. Making the reminder signs was a good first step, but I have to be committed – not just interested – in making No Matter What a habit in all areas of my life."

"Great, Ryan," said Jeff, standing and extending his hand. "I look forward to seeing you next Tuesday."

As soon as I got into my car, I wrote in my notebook:

... And Then Some

Key Points:

✔ My attitude is important, but I need to change my habits as well.

✔ And Then Some is not necessarily something big. It is making a habit of consistently doing the seemingly small things.

✔ Anyone at any level in any position can give lagniappe.

✔ I may find myself traveling "the extra mile" alone, but that is where real success happens.

✔ No more blaming or justifying why I am where I am. It is time to move forward.

My Assignment: Learn success truths from receptionist.

Do Something Different:

1. Be committed.

2. Develop an And Then Some habit by actively looking for ways to go the extra mile or give some lagniappe – both at work and at home.

The Third Tuesday

Consider It Done

For our third meeting, I arrived at Jeff's promptly at 7:00 a.m. As usual, he greeted me at the door with a warm handshake before leading me to the table and chairs on the back deck where our coffee was waiting for us. While the weather was gorgeous and the view as amazing as ever, something seemed different. I finally decided it was Jeff – for some reason, he wasn't his usual, upbeat self.

"You okay?" I asked.

"I'm fine, thanks," he responded, settling into his chair. "When we began our Tuesday morning meetings, I told you the reason we needed to commit to eight weeks was because during that period a lot of 'life' would happen to you. Remember?"

"Sure I do. I also remember you saying that some things might happen that would test my commitment," I added. "And you said I would see some of life's curveballs thrown my way."

"That's right ... and I also said some of those curveballs might come my direction as well. Well, yesterday, I was thrown a curveball. My son, Mark, called me to let me know he was ready to quit his job. I'm not sure what's going on in his life, but that move is way out of character for him. So I cancelled my schedule for the remainder of the week and will be catching a flight to go see him later today."

I could see Jeff's concern for his son. "Do you want to reschedule today's meeting or next week's meeting?" I offered.

"Absolutely not!" he retorted. "I promise, you will have my full and undivided attention today and next Tuesday, as always. These meetings are good for both of us. You see, I learn at least as much from them as you do. When I spend time thinking about and preparing for our meetings, it reinforces my own beliefs and shows me what I need to work on and improve. And each curveball in life gives us yet another opportunity to practice the simple truths of success.

"When I talk to Mark, I hope I will be able to draw from our meetings. If I were a gambler, I'd bet that he hasn't quite wrapped his head around the No Matter What lesson that we've talked about at length. As I've told you, no problem is unique to you. And whatever Mark's issues are, they are not unique to him. I'm just glad he asked me to come visit him and help him work through them ...," Jeff hesitated, "before he resigns."

He then paused for a moment, which was his way of refocusing. "So, Ryan, were you able to visit with Julie last week?" he said, finally.

Jeff couldn't know how much I'd been looking forward to this conversation. "Well, last week when I left here, I thought you were a little off base, asking me to meet with our receptionist. In my mind I thought, *What does she know about success – she's just a receptionist?* She's not someone I considered to be on a challenging career path. But, given the fact that I had committed to you that I would complete the homework assignments, I followed through.

"Jeff, you were absolutely on point. What I discovered was mind-boggling as well as humbling. Julie, whom I'd never taken the time to get to know, is an extremely intelligent and interesting person. One of the first things I found out was that she knows you quite well. You didn't tell me you knew Julie, so I'm thinking you sort of set me up on this one, didn't you?"

"Not really," Jeff grinned. "I wasn't sure she was still there, but I have to admit I was glad when you said the receptionist's name was Julie. I knew if it was the same Julie I'd worked with, she would be a great resource for you … and as I'm sure you quickly learned, she is a very special person as well as being quite good at her job.

"I went to Julie for advice many times. She always had a finger on the pulse of the organization and what was happening with the business." It was obvious Jeff respected Julie's opinions. "Her career path was defined by her personal values. She chose to remain the receptionist, even though I attempted to promote her several times. Julie loved her work and was only interested in being the best receptionist in the country. I don't know about your experience, but in my eyes, she accomplished that goal ... And Then Some," he finished with a smile.

"So how did your meeting with her go?" he asked.

"I took her to lunch as you suggested. When I told her you were coaching me, she said to make sure and tell you 'hello.' She also said you were one of the very few executives who truly knew the power of the receptionist."

"She does have power," Jeff agreed. "She is the eyes and ears for everything that goes on, and she is the first impression of the company for every person who comes through the door. So, tell me, what did you learn from Julie?"

"Well, I asked her what she thought were the key characteristics of the successful people she had worked with through the years," I began. "And she said, in her opinion, there were three things that successful people did differently from the rest of the pack.

"First, she said the most successful people were the ones who had an 'abundance mentality.' These people believe there is plenty of knowledge, wisdom and success for everyone. In other words, there is room for everyone to be successful – one person's success does not diminish or reduce the possibility of another person's success.

"Related to that is the second characteristic," I continued. "Julie said she's observed that successful people are open-minded enough to ask for others' input and be willing to learn from it. She said you were a great example of a leader

who learned from everyone and was threatened by no one …
and when you retired from the organization, nobody asked
for her opinion again for a long time. She also said people
have tried to fill your shoes since then, but every person has
allowed their ego and arrogance to get in the way of good
common sense. In her opinion, they were afraid to ask others
what changes needed to be made to improve.

"In fact, she reminded me of a situation I'd completely
forgotten about. About a year after you left the company,
upper management came out with a directive to change our
business hours. They thought it would be better for our
customers and employees. But they didn't ask for anyone's
input before they came out with the big news. When they
proudly announced the change, you could see every frontline
employee grimace. They knew it wouldn't work … and it didn't.

"Julie pointed out that if upper management had just asked,
they would have discovered there were good reasons why the
hours were what they were. Julie and other employees had
the knowledge to share but weren't asked," I said, adding,
"That's a waste of resources."

I checked my notes and then said, "Julie said something that
really stuck with me: People in the organization have the
answers most of the time if the right questions are asked. In
fact, people will drown you with good ideas if you just ask them.

"The third key characteristic was 'follow-through.' Julie felt
strongly that most people do not follow through and do what
they say they're going to do. They may do part of what they
say, but rarely do they do all of what they promise. According
to Julie, this probably isn't intentional, nor does she think

people deliberately lie. But the fact remains: They don't follow through … and because of this shortcoming, their integrity is always in question.

I paused. "Jeff, she said you were different because you cared enough to ask questions – you even asked the receptionist – and that you could be depended on to do what you said. That's some pretty good wisdom from a person I hadn't taken the time to get to know because I thought that she was 'just the receptionist.'"

Jeff smiled at my last statement. "I'm pleased your meeting went well and that she remembered me. Now, let me tell you why I always admired Julie. When she took the job, I was frustrated because many of the people in our organization did things halfway. The reason I hired her was because she appeared to be a wonderful person whose attitude was positive, energetic and upbeat.

"Her first day on the job, I asked her to do a small, insignificant first assignment," Jeff continued. "After she understood what I wanted, as she was leaving my office, she said to me, 'Consider it done!'

"*Hey … that's a great attitude*, I thought, but I was skeptical. I figured it was nothing more than nice words. You know, the new employee trying to impress the boss. However, much to my surprise and delight, those three simple words reflected her dependability and confidence, not just in that instance but again and again. Sure enough, the next time I saw her, the project was done – on time and exactly the way I had asked her to do it."

Jeff went on, "After that day, I started thinking about her words, 'Consider it done!' What if my entire organization thought the same way? What if everyone either considered it done when they accepted an assignment or project or, right up front, raised their concerns so we could figure out why it couldn't be done in the time or manner being requested?

"Those three simple words that came from Julie – Consider It Done – became a guiding principle within our organization. From that day forward, every person on our team began doing all that needed to be done – no more jobs done halfway. Occasionally we had to re-negotiate the project up front, but most of the time we would walk away and Consider It Done with confidence.

"I remember several times when we did what we referred to as a 'sanity check,'" Jeff said. "We outlined on a white board exactly what had to take place to accomplish the project. That way all of us could clearly see if what we were trying to do was feasible or not. If it wasn't, we had to adjust our timing or our expectations. After doing that, we could leave the room knowing that everyone could Consider It Done."

As he placed his coffee mug on the table, Jeff said, "Julie taught me that people are looking for consistency. They want to know that the values won't change based on the situation of the day. Her words – Consider It Done – made a tremendous impact on my success and the success of our organization. I'll tell you, Ryan, that was a turning point in my career."

"Why are those simple words – Consider It Done – so powerful?" I wondered aloud.

"There are more than words within that phrase," Jeff was quick to respond. "There is confidence, commitment and accountability ... plus, it reflects an attitude of moving forward. Committing to those three words is the test of our integrity – the master switch, if you will, that controls every other part of success.

"You see, when a person sacrifices his integrity, nothing else really matters," he said almost sadly. "Does it matter what you say if no one trusts you? Does it matter how committed, skilled, courageous or optimistic you are if people do not believe you? I can tell you, Ryan, none of those traits matter if people can't listen to what you say and Consider It Done.

"People who live by the Consider It Done principle possess one of the most respected virtues in all of life, and that virtue is integrity. People want to be with others whose audio (that is, their words) is in sync with their video (their actions). If you have proven yourself to be honest and trustworthy and you can be counted on to deliver on your word, you are indeed a unique and valued person."

I was writing in my notebook as fast as I could as Jeff's words echoed in my head.

"Sounds pretty simple, right?" he continued. "Yet loss of integrity – primarily due to arrogance and ego – is the principal reason for failure. Look at the people who make the news every evening because of some scandal – sports figures, film stars, politicians, CEOs. What they all have in common is that, somewhere along the way, they lost their integrity."

Then, he surprised me with a question. "How would you define integrity, Ryan?"

I put down my pen and thought for a moment. "I guess the simplest definition is doing what you say you are going to do," I replied. "Or as Julie would say, Consider It Done!"

"Good," he nodded. "Many people have a difficult time defining integrity. They know it when they see it, but like most intangible qualities, it's really tough to describe.

"Not long ago, integrity was the single most searched-for word on Merriam-Webster's Dictionary Web site, which implies that a lot of people aren't exactly sure what integrity means," Jeff explained. "Everyone knows it's important to be a person of integrity, but most do not know exactly what the word means.

"Many people use the words 'integrity' and 'honesty' interchangeably. Integrity is a much broader term, coming from the word 'integral,' which means 'whole or undivided,'" he said. "If you have integrity, you are a complete person … without it, you're fragmented and incomplete.

"My personal definition of integrity means never being ashamed of my reflection," Jeff confided. "If you can look in the mirror every day without regret, your integrity is in check."

I quickly nodded because I knew exactly what he meant.

"When I was growing up," Jeff paused to look squarely into my eyes, "my parents took the time to be really clear about the importance of integrity," he continued. "They taught me that the worst thing I could ever lose was my reputation. In our house, we never had to define integrity. We just had to identify what we thought was the right thing to do.

"In fact, every time I brought an issue to my dad, the first question he would ask was, 'Son, what do you think is the right thing to do?' Of course, I hated that question at the time. But after many years of reflection, I came to realize that answering that question would clarify and cement the action I needed to take."

"But it seems like 'the right thing' isn't always black and white," I observed.

"I'll be the first to acknowledge that sometimes it's difficult to know what is the right thing to do," Jeff agreed. "That's when we have to clear our mind so we can figure out what is 'right.'"

Jeff thought for a minute. "It's sort of like when you install new software on your computer. Once loaded, it automatically runs what is called an 'integrity check,' a series of tests to determine if any part of the program has been lost or damaged. If any piece of the code in that program doesn't have complete integrity, the program as a whole can't be trusted. At best, you would have a program that wasn't functioning properly. At worst, using a program lacking integrity could cause you to lose valuable data or even damage your computer. The integrity check is vital.

"When faced with a situation, we can also run an integrity check," Jeff explained. "Our integrity check is to ask ourselves, 'What is the right thing to do?' If we're honest with ourselves, we'll know the answer.

"Think about some of the huge organizations that have fallen because of integrity issues. Where would they be today if someone had answered the question, 'What is the right thing to do?'" Jeff wondered. "Would Enron's path have led to destruction, or would they still be an inspirational success story? Would WorldCom or Arthur Andersen still have thousands on their payrolls? Would Bernie Madoff have swindled more than 14,000 clients for over $50 billion if someone within his organization had the nerve to ask him, 'Are we doing the right thing?' Would the financial meltdown of subprime mortgages have happened if borrowers, lenders, underwriters – or anyone else – had bothered to ask and answer the question, 'What is the right thing to do?' Of course not!"

I could see that these glaring losses of corporate and personal integrity were actually painful for Jeff to think about.

"Ryan, I won't ask you to do this often," he continued, "but I want you to write this down, word for word: Integrity is the commitment to do what is right, regardless of the circumstances.

"Got it," I said.

"Good," Jeff continued, "Now, what does 'regardless' mean to you?"

I thought for a few seconds and then responded, "To me, 'regardless' means 'in any event.' Or maybe, No Matter What."

"Exactly!" Jeff was getting wound up. "You have to keep your integrity No Matter What. If people don't trust you, they will not want to be around you. Developing trust depends entirely upon the integrity you consistently demonstrate. But in reality, many people spend more time polishing their image than living up to their word. They are more concerned with how they look than what they are doing."

Jeff then asked a rhetorical question: "But who are they trying to fool?

"Here's something to think about and remember," he went on. "You cannot straddle integrity. You are either on one side or the other ... and you have to be consistent. No hidden agendas, no political games.

"Our success comes from our ability to use our common sense, listen to others and be consistent in our actions," Jeff summarized. "I attribute a large part of my success to learning and applying Julie's three simple words to everything I do."

"Consider It Done," I repeated, not realizing I had said it aloud.

"Precisely. Believe me, those are powerful words everyone wants to hear and believe," Jeff said as he looked at his watch. "Ryan, I've spent most of our hour talking ... and just so you know, I've been talking to myself just as much as I've been talking to you. You know, we all wrestle with our integrity and living up to Julie's simple Consider It Done principle, and this morning has been a good reminder for me."

"I have to admit that I really didn't think I would learn much from our receptionist," I confessed again. "But, as you mentioned, success is all around us if we ask the right questions. This has been a good session for me, too, and I hope your visit with your son goes well."

"Thanks, Ryan. But just because I'm leaving town doesn't let you off the hook," Jeff said with a wink. "Here's the assignment I had in mind. During the remainder of the week, I want you to take some time to reflect on the three simple truths we've covered so far: No Matter What, And Then Some, and Consider It Done. And then I want you to take it one step further and jot down any situations where you might not be following through as well as you could be.

"One more question," Jeff said. "About how much time did it take for you to meet with Julie and Kelley?"

"Let's see …," I paused as I added up the time in my head. "If you count drive time and meeting time, the total was about two hours for each of them."

Jeff stood and extended his hand. "That's about what I thought. This week I want you to take two hours and dedicate that time to your wife, Michele. The time needs to be dedicated exclusively to her – no television, not at mealtime – but dedicated time with Michele. I want you to begin working on your marriage while we are working together on your professional life. I suggest you begin by telling her about our first three meetings and see if you two can apply the same principles to your home life."

"Good idea," I said. Spending uninterrupted time together was something that was missing in our relationship. "I've shared a little about our meetings with her, but we have not taken the time to talk about how we can apply these simple truths to our home life. Thanks for the suggestion. I look forward to our meeting next Tuesday. And Jeff ... safe travels."

As I walked to my car, I could tell Jeff was hurting for his son. I wished I had more to offer in the way of comfort.

When I reached the car, I pulled out my notebook. As I jotted down my assignment, I realized Jeff hadn't asked what I would do differently this week. I thought for a few minutes about the meeting we'd just had, and then finished my notes.

Consider It Done

Key Points:

✔ Successful people have an abundance mentality. The keys to success are all around me if I pay attention and listen.

✔ Consider It Done – do what you say you will do.

✔ Integrity is never being ashamed of my reflection.

✔ Success comes from our ability to use our common sense, listen to others and be consistent in our actions.

My Assignment:

1. Spend quality time with Michele.

2. Reflect specifically on how I can apply the three simple truths – No Matter What, And Then Some, and Consider It Done – in my work and in my life.

Do Something Different:

1. Act with integrity No Matter What.

2. Act so that when I say I'll do something, others can Consider It Done.

3. Use an Integrity Check by asking: "What is the right thing to do?"

The Fourth Tuesday

Above All Else

As I drove out to the lake early the next Tuesday, I wondered how Jeff's visit had gone with his son Mark. During our last session, I could tell he was anxious about what was going on in Mark's life, and I hoped everything had worked out well. But today I also was excited about sharing the results of my assignment with Jeff.

He met me at the door with his usual smile and cup of coffee.

"Hello, Ryan. Thanks for being on time again. I appreciate your promptness," Jeff said. "You know, that's an important trait many people overlook. When folks are late, it is disrespectful and an insult to the person they are meeting. In my book, promptness would fall into the simple truth of Consider It Done. Anyway, I'm preaching to the choir …

"So, tell me ... how was your week?"

"Without going into too much detail, I'll tell you I made some significant progress at home this week," I began. "I spent two hours – And Then Some – of dedicated time with Michele. It was the first time we'd sat down and talked, uninterrupted, in a long time. I was eager to share the details of our three meetings and the simple truths you've taught me. You were right, of course ... taking notes in this notebook was a great idea. I was able to pull it out and show Michele specifics."

I took a breath before continuing. "We talked about how we could apply the truths to our marriage, and we made a commitment to each other to implement the lessons I'd learned so far. We thought we'd done okay in the And Then Some category but knew we needed to work on the others.

"First, we decided that we needed to accept responsibility for where we are financially. Last year was bad for us with the economy, but we realized that we have to move forward No Matter What to address the problem. We also talked about how casy it is for each of us to get wrapped up in our careers and let some personal things slip through the cracks. But those things are just as important as work. So from here on out, if we agree that a personal commitment is important and reasonable, we will Consider It Done.

"Jeff, I want to thank you for suggesting the dedicated time with Michele. She is my best friend, but the amount of time I'd been spending with her didn't reflect that. I'd rationalized that the quality of our time together was more important than the quantity of our time together. What I discovered this week is that we both need quality and quantity. Nothing makes me feel better than laughing with Michele, and nothing makes her feel better than laughing with me.

"So, we decided that spending time together would be the number one priority of our marriage, and we outlined how we are going to do that. Some of the things we agreed to could be game-changers in our marriage."

"That's great, Ryan." Jeff seemed sincerely happy I'd shared the simple truths with Michele. "I'm glad to hear things went so well. You know, the causes of most marital problems are the same as business problems – communication and misperceptions. So I hope you will continue to make communicating with Michele a priority. It will make a big difference."

Jeff rubbed his palms together. "Now, what about at work? Any changes?"

"Yep!" I said smiling. "I definitely made progress there, as well. I've created a No Matter What philosophy of my own … that I will no longer justify, blame or provide excuses for anything that goes on in my life. Putting it simply, my number one priority is to accept responsibility – No Matter What – and move forward."

Again, Jeff looked pleased.

"I've also implemented an And Then Some strategy for myself … kind of like Gerald Stokes did. If a cab driver can separate himself from the competition by doing a little something extra, I can as well. For instance, at work I held a meeting and asked my team to come up with some ideas for how we can offer And Then Some services in our organization. I was thrilled with their suggestions but also a little chagrined when one person said that my asking for their opinion was an example of And Then Some. As simple as it sounds, just asking for an opinion was adding value. I think Kelley and Julie would have cringed if they'd heard what this person said.

"The third commitment I've made is to become a person of my word by living Julie's Consider It Done philosophy. As we talked last week, if people don't believe me, it doesn't matter what I say. I have to be true to myself and to my word. In the past, I'm not sure that people would have said about me, 'We can Consider It Done.' I know it will take some time to win back the trust of people whom I've let down in the past, but I'm willing to work hard to see their trust in me restored.

"Reflecting on the simple truths you've shared forced me to acknowledge that I'd become complacent ... without even realizing it. And I think that's a large part of the reason I'm in this rut," I concluded.

"Ryan, those are great applications of the simple truths we've covered so far," he said. "And I think you'll find every one of those truths will help you re-discover who you are and where you need to be going.

"I listened with interest when you said you'd become complacent. Complacency is the root of mediocrity, and mediocrity is success's worst enemy – a far greater enemy, in fact, than failure. If viewed with the right perspective, failure leads to success because it forces you to move in another direction. Mediocrity, on the other hand, hinders success because it keeps us in our comfort zone with excuses and false beliefs, preventing us from doing what we need to do to move forward."

"I think you're right, Jeff. No doubt, it's tough to move forward when you are complacent. 'Complacency is the root of mediocrity' ... I have to remember that." I paused for a moment. "Not to change the subject, but I'm eager to hear how it went with Mark last week."

"The bottom line is that things are going to be okay," Jeff said, although I noticed he wasn't smiling ... nor was he grimacing, either. "Mark called me because he was ready to quit his job. Everyone gets to that point at one time or another, but to bail out without a plan is really out of character for Mark.

"The issue with Mark is that he is less than a year into a two-year contract, and he has recently discovered things are not exactly the way they were represented in his interviews," Jeff explained. "Now, there is nothing illegal going on ... just some issues with his boss."

Jeff took another sip of coffee. "Tell me, Ryan. Do you think Mark is the first person to have a problem with his boss?" His expression was mostly serious, but I also detected a gleam in his eyes.

"Umm ... I don't think so!" I laughed with Jeff. "I've had some issues with a few of my bosses ... and I imagine people on my team have had some issues with me as well."

"Of course. It's natural to have some challenges with your boss from time to time," Jeff said. "This is Mark's first job and the first of many situations – and lessons – he will learn that are a little different than those he studied in his college textbooks.

"Anyway, this week provided me an opportunity to talk with Mark about the simple truths that you and I have been discussing, as well as the ones we'll be talking about during the rest of our coaching sessions. So I was grateful that he called, and I enjoyed our time together," Jeff said.

"I also think he is back on track to fulfill his two-year commitment. As I said, the issues Mark is working through with his boss are not illegal, immoral or unethical," he continued. "It's like most other issues … simply a misunderstanding. The way he described his boss – demanding, driven and focused – sounds like some of the most successful people I know. He thinks that she allows her job to consume all of her life and that she expects the same from him. Of course, he hasn't talked about his concerns with her. No, he just thought it might be best for him to quit and find another job that was more aligned with what he thought was best for him.

"I'll confess, though," Jeff confided. "I was tempted to jump across the dining room table and shake some sense into him when he told me that. Mark has a good job – and as you know, good jobs are not easy to get these days. He has a two-year agreement, and halfway through he was ready to bail out? This was nonsense! But I needed to act like a mature father and hear him out."

I chuckled to myself, wondering if I could have kept my cool like Jeff had done.

"When you make a commitment to a person or an organization, you have to be 'all in,'" Jeff explained. "I think that Mark was 'half in,' just trying to get by. If he'd been giving his all, he would have been communicating with his boss all along. I told him that I've known a lot of people who regretted just trying to get by. But in my entire career, I've never heard anyone say they regretted giving it their all ... even if it didn't work out."

Jeff paused to take another sip of coffee. "I shared with Mark that, at this point in his career, perhaps the most important guiding principle is that he adhere to his values 'Above All Else.' Above All Else means you understand what the most important, non-negotiable things in your job and your life really are.

"When I began talking to Mark about adhering to his values, Above All Else, he admitted that he hadn't specifically identified anything he would say was non-negotiable in his life."

"So," I interrupted to ask, "if nothing is non-negotiable and if you haven't clearly defined your values, then everything is up for negotiation?"

"Precisely," Jeff answered. "For instance, when I asked Mark what his employment contract meant to him, he said it was for his protection. His protection? What about the organization that signed the agreement? That contract is for the protection of both parties ... and if he was willing to bail out on his end, why shouldn't he expect the same from his company? They both made a commitment and that commitment should be Above All Else.

"Mark also has to learn that you do not leave, abandon or bail out of a problem. That's the coward's way out," Jeff emphasized. "It's very rare that someone comes out better when they leave a problem. For example, I've known many people who left an organization because of some problem or issue. They find another 'opportunity,' but soon discover the same problem exists at the new organization. Rather than pursuing a valid opportunity, they were really running away from a problem.

"So, I'll say it as concisely as I can: Never leave a problem – work to resolve it instead – and move toward genuine opportunity."

Jeff paused to take another sip of coffee. "So … back to Above All Else … when you develop, express and live values that are Above All Else, you can change not only yourself but an entire organization. Take Southwest Airlines, one of the most successful airlines in the world. Southwest was established with a guiding principle of 'employee first.' Since its existence, Southwest has taken care of its employees, Above All Else.

"Recently, when the economy got tough, Southwest employees were able to repay their employer. During the most financially challenging time in the history of the airline industry, Southwest Airlines' employees voluntarily forfeited $5 million in vacation time and $1 million in pay to help the company stay afloat.

"Employees also took over the lawn and facility maintenance at corporate headquarters," Jeff recounted. "These employees were simply reflecting the deep commitment – personal and professional – they felt they received from their company. If Southwest's leadership had not established their values Above

All Else, they probably would have made different decisions and wouldn't have provided their team the opportunity to pitch in and help.

"Ryan, I've seen many people and organizations overreact to the next hot deal, new slogan, cutting-edge philosophy and fresh management concept without establishing the guiding values they would put Above All Else. In essence, they keep creating the next new 'Above All Else,' which means that they don't have a guiding philosophy at all.

"Another example of a company that lives its values Above All Else is Chick-fil-A. Are you familiar with that incredibly successful fast-food company?" Jeff asked.

"Yes, of course," I answered. "Chick-fil-A is one of my favorite places to grab a quick bite. Their chicken sandwich is the best."

Jeff went on, "In the highly competitive fast-food business, Chick-fil-A has made a stand: Their restaurants will not be open on Sundays. Conventional wisdom says that's a ridiculous policy because Sunday is a big day for fast food.

"Truett Cathey, who founded Chick-fil-A, believed that for six days his employees work and on the seventh, they rest. Any question about what is Above All Else at Chick-fil-A? By the way, they also are a good example of And Then Some. Every person in their organization has been trained not only to serve their customers, but also respond to any customer request by saying, every time, 'It's my pleasure.' Those simple words reinforce their commitment to the people who buy their products."

"I know their service is outstanding ... just like their food," I interjected.

Jeff nodded his agreement. "The Chick-fil-A philosophy is that you have to re-earn your reputation every day. They know that if your people understand what the company's values are Above All Else, they will give their customers great service ... And Then Some. Those customers, in turn, will become repeat customers."

"No argument here," I said.

"In Mark's case, he's learning that his personal values will ultimately guide his professional career," Jeff said, adding, "I have to remind myself often of the most important things in my life as well, so I know sometimes it's not easy to keep those values in crystal-clear focus."

Jeff excused himself and returned momentarily with hot warm-ups for our coffee. "I know it's been several weeks ... but when we took a tour of the house, did you notice the Above All Else plaque in my office?"

I thought for a moment, searching my memory. "Yes, I believe so. It was sitting alone under that beautiful picture with the caption, 'Values ... know them, believe them, live them.' I didn't get the connection at the time, but now I think I understand."

Jeff said, "Those words, 'Above All Else,' remind me to remain calm and level-headed, even in the midst of economic, personal or business turmoil. The one thing that should never change is our values. They should be Above All Else.

To me, Above All Else means I precisely understand my values and know – without a doubt – that I will not compromise them, regardless of the situation. Ryan, this is one of the most important simple truths we will discuss."

I nodded as I jotted down some of the keywords Jeff was sharing.

Jeff continued. "I once knew a man named Don who worked for an appraisal company. His job was to provide property appraisals based on recent sales in the area and on his knowledge of the market. He was very good at his job and enjoyed what he did. When the real estate market went south, his boss pressured him to appraise high or low, depending on the situation, or potentially lose his job.

"But Don is a man of courage and integrity. He decided not to compromise his values and refused to manipulate his appraisals. So he quit. He stepped out in faith and began his own appraisal company, even though his market timing could not have been much worse. After struggling through the start-up, his business prospered. His company is now successful and is based on the values he would not sacrifice in his previous job.

"Don knew he really had no choice. He had chosen the values by which he would live his life Above All Else," Jeff concluded. "Ultimately, the true measure of success is being able to look in the mirror and know that you had the courage to live the values that are Above All Else in your life."

"Wow," I said. "That is a powerful story."

"Yes, it is," Jeff agreed. And then he leaned forward and said,

"Ryan, this is real-world stuff – a conflict in values, a bad time to be looking for a job. That's why you have to know what is Above All Else and non-negotiable in your life."

Pausing for a moment to collect his thoughts, Jeff continued. "Back to Mark for a minute … something else I shared with him is that most people have a natural tendency to exaggerate the good things – and the bad things – going on in their lives. In reality, the bad is never as bad as it seems, and the good is never as good as it seems. Later, Mark admitted that he had exaggerated the bad in his work life."

"I'm guilty of exaggerating the good and bad as well," I admitted.

"Me too," Jeff concurred. "It's a natural response, and I have to constantly remind myself not to exaggerate the reality of the situation. One of the ways I keep myself in check is to remind myself that 'this too shall pass.' Have you ever heard that phrase?"

"Of course," I said. "My mother used to tell me that a lot, although I haven't thought of it much since my youth."

"Actually, I'm not sure where the saying 'this too shall pass' originated," he confessed. "But Abraham Lincoln shared the following story in 1859." Jeff pulled out a sheet of paper with one paragraph on it, handed it across the table and asked me to read it.

I cleared my throat and read: "It is said an Eastern monarch once charged his wise men to invent him a sentence, to be ever in view, and which should be true and appropriate in all times and situations. Eventually the wise men presented the king with the words: 'And this too shall pass away.'"

Jeff immediately reinforced what I'd read. "Those words give us hope that, regardless of what we're going through, it is temporary. I think I can attribute much of my success to two things: my unquestionable set of values Above All Else and the knowledge that 'this too shall pass.'

"My Above All Else philosophy is not the beginning or the ending. It's just one more simple truth to help in your quest for success," Jeff concluded.

We simultaneously looked at our watches ... and then laughed at the unplanned synchronicity.

"We are about out of time, as you are noticing," Jeff joked. "So tell me. What did you learn today that you can do differently?"

"One change I have to make is to be clearer in my values," I began. "I think I know what I would put Above All Else, but I need to write them down. I also learned from Mark and Don's experiences that my personal values will guide my professional career. Mark, who hadn't yet established his personal values, was just reacting to a crisis he was facing without having a moral compass to guide him in the right direction. Don, whose moral compass was clear and without question, knew exactly what was Above All Else and reacted accordingly.

"So before our meeting next week, I want to spend some time identifying what is Above All Else for me," I finished.

"Great. Couldn't have said it better." Jeff stood and shook my hand. "You're a quick study, just as I remembered."

"Before our next meeting, I'd like you to pay a visit to a friend of mine, Jerry Ferguson. Here is his number. He's a football coach with an unbelievable winning streak, so he must be doing something better than his competitors. I told him you'd be calling to make an appointment with him. When you two get together, listen for what he considers to be the reasons for his success," Jeff counseled. "You may be surprised to hear what he has to say."

"I'm excited," I admitted, "and I'll be listening. I've followed Coach Ferguson's success in the media, so I'm looking forward to meeting him and hearing what he says separates his teams from the others. Thank you for arranging a meeting with him."

Once I was back in my car, I wrote in my notebook:

Above All Else

Key Points:

✔ Complacency is the root of mediocrity.

✔ Above All Else means I understand – without question – what is non-negotiable in my job and in my life.

✔ When you make a commitment, you have to be "all in."

✔ This too shall pass.

✔ Most people have a natural tendency to exaggerate the good things and the bad things going on in their lives.

My Assignment:

1. Learn success truths from Coach Ferguson.

2. Identify and write down what is non-negotiable and Above All Else for me.

Do Something Different:

1. Never leave a problem – instead, move toward an opportunity.

2. Know my values, believe them, live them.

The Fifth Tuesday

From Now On ...

By this time, I was eagerly awaiting my Tuesday Mornings with Jeff. He had a knack for sharing wisdom in a way that made his advice immediately actionable. I'd already made several changes that were having a positive impact on both my personal and professional life. I could confidently say I'd quit digging my rut deeper and, hopefully, would be out of it completely before long.

I pulled into Jeff's driveway well before our meeting time. When I rang the bell, he was as congenial as always. We grabbed two steaming hot cups of coffee from the kitchen and went directly to the deck.

"How are things going, Ryan?" he asked. "Were you able to see Jerry Ferguson?"

"Yes. I met with Coach Ferguson last Wednesday evening," I said, "and we had a great time. Your ears must have been burning that night because we talked about you a lot. The coach admires what you have achieved, but he respects, even more, the way you've achieved it."

Jeff smiled. "Coach Ferguson's success is legendary. I appreciate his comments, but I learned a lot from him. You see, he was my high school football coach. Did he share that with you?"

"Yes, he did. He said you were a great player but didn't have the natural ability many of your teammates had. The coach said you studied every opponent and knew what they were going to do before they did it. He also remembered that you were able to stay calm and make good choices in the heat of the battle. That's why you made All State. I didn't know you were such a gridiron star."

"That was a long time ago and doesn't seem as significant now as it once was. But, I learned a lot from my high school and college coaches that I've been able to use in my career. Anyway, how did the rest of the week go?"

"Ironically, I took my kids to eat at Chick-fil-A twice and flew on Southwest Airlines when I made a daytrip at the end of the week. In both settings, I was more keenly aware of the people I came into contact with. One thing I noticed is that every person who took care of me in both places seemed to actually care about my experience.

"Oh, and while I was eating at Chick-fil-A, I saw a plaque that said, 'Associate yourselves only with those people you can be proud of – whether they work for you or you work for them.'

That's pretty good advice in and of itself. I also was told, 'It's my pleasure' at least three times during my two visits. I had to smile every time I heard that phrase.

"On Southwest," I continued, "I looked around for evidence of And Then Some service, and it didn't take me long to find it. It was Valentine's Day, and they gave out candy, treats and prizes. I thoroughly enjoyed their lagniappe. Smiles and laughs were abundant in their waiting area, a place where most passengers are stressed out.

"I also noticed how the flight attendants maintained their positive attitudes No Matter What, amid screaming babies and kids everywhere. It's been a while since I paid attention to the flight attendants. On most airlines, I try to avoid being dragged down by their usually sour attitudes. The Southwest pilots even had an And Then Some attitude – they left the cockpit after we landed and stood on the jet bridge, thanking the passengers as they got off the plane. It was interesting to see some of your simple truths in action.

"Before I tell you about my meeting with Coach Ferguson," I went on, "I've been curious ... did anything happen at Mark's work during the week?"

"Mark called last night," Jeff said. "He has a meeting set up with his boss today to discuss his frustrations. I'm almost sure it will all work out okay. As I may have mentioned, we spent quite a bit of time during my visit discussing that it is his responsibility to manage his relationship with his boss. Regardless of the kind of boss she is, Mark should not expect her to carry the entire load.

"So, we'll see. He's supposed to call me tonight and let me know how it went. Unless something disastrous happens, he's not going to quit, thank goodness. I'll be sure to let you know what happens.

"May I ask how you coached Mark with respect to how he should approach his boss?" I asked. "I'd think that could be sort of tricky."

"Yes, it could be tricky … if he wasn't prepared," Jeff said. "I told him he should approach the issue with his boss just like he would approach any other problem he encounters in business. First, clearly identify the problem. Most people jump to a solution before they understand precisely what the problem is. As a result, they solve the wrong problem. That is what I suspect Mark had been doing – trying to solve a problem that didn't exist, while allowing the real problem to pick up steam."

"How do you know if you're solving the right problem?" I questioned, knowing I'd been guilty of jumping to conclusions in the past.

"Good question," Jeff smiled. "I think the key is to write down three things:

1. The problem as you perceive it;

2. The impact it has on you or others; and

3. What you want to accomplish – your desired end state.

"Once you've gone through those three steps, you have everything you need to begin looking for solutions to the problem. Next, write down:

4. Why you think the problem exists; and

5. Potential solutions.

"You'll be surprised how often new options surface when you know exactly what the problem is, its impact, and what you'd like to accomplish," Jeff continued. "And if you're going to talk to someone about an issue, you definitely want to offer some potential solutions. Just walking in and throwing out a problem without any plan or suggestion won't get most people very far."

"Good point," I concurred.

"In Mark's case, he perceives the issue to be that his boss does not make her expectations clear. The impact on Mark is that he is left to set his own priorities, and on many occasions, his priorities have not been in sync with hers. This has created conflict between the two of them and led to some run-ins, and that was why Mark was frustrated and wanted to quit.

"After we talked, Mark understood that what he wants is to clearly understand his boss's expectations of and priorities for him. He thinks the problem came about because they are short-handed, and there's so much work to be done that everyone is focused on the urgent rather than the important. (By the way, we'll talk more about identifying priorities in a few weeks.)

"His proposed solution is that they meet weekly for just 10 minutes to clarify priorities and expectations.

"Now, when he talks with his boss, he'll be able to clearly identify the problem as he perceives it, the problem's impact on him and his work, how he would like their relationship to work and some alternative solutions."

"That makes sense," I said as I quickly made a few notes. "And good advice. Thanks."

"So, back to this past week," Jeff redirected the conversation. "What did you learn from Coach Ferguson?"

"Well, as you know, the coach is an amazing man. Thanks for setting up our meeting," I said, hoping Jeff sensed not only my excitement about speaking with Coach Ferguson, but also my gratitude for the opportunity.

"I met with him after he made a presentation at a coach's clinic that afternoon. He began our meeting by telling me his presentation that day was about how to survive and enjoy high-school coaching. I thought that was pretty interesting, because one thing I'm discovering through this process is that people are willing to share their experience, knowledge, passion and wisdom … if they are asked. Their 'secrets' aren't really secrets. Julie, the receptionist, opened my eyes to that a couple of weeks ago. Most successful people want to help others be successful, too. In fact, they are often an open book of wisdom, if asked.

"Anyway," I continued, "when he walked into the room, it seemed to literally light up. His contagious smile, rugged looks and obvious confidence made an awesome first impression. It's hard not to be overwhelmed by his presence. He immediately made a connection with me when he asked about my work, my family, my relationship with you, and what I had discovered so far in our coaching sessions.

"I filled in the blanks for him and told him one of the most interesting things I'd learned was that all the people I'd talked to had different 'most important' simple truths of success. However, they all agreed that success was more than just doing one thing well. Then I asked Coach if there was one particular guiding principle he thought had contributed to his success.

"He thanked me for asking and said he was honored to be included in our sessions," I shared. "Then he told me that his success was preceded by his most devastating failure: When he was a young coach, he thought he was invincible and could win every game. But his first year, he didn't win a game – not one. He said the boosters were ready to cut their losses and let him go. The truth became obvious to him and everyone else – he was not invincible.

"He was vulnerable to failure ... just like everyone else," I said, stopping to flip to the next page in my notes.

"At that point – his lowest of lows – he discovered his greatest success principle: 'From Now On.' You see, his choices were either to quit or to pick himself up and move forward. He chose to pick himself up, and he made himself a promise: From that point on, he would learn from his failures, and he would not make the same mistake twice. So, his success principle is simply stated: 'From Now On ....'

"Coach said it's okay to fail – everyone fails at some point – but it's not okay to keep failing," I remembered.

"He also said one of the main reasons people continue to fail is that they are reluctant to face the truth, just as he was," I explained. "His record was his record – zero wins – but he wanted his record to be better so badly, he began trying to avoid reality. He said he kept making things up to maintain the alignment of his hopes with his dreams. For example, he said he tried to justify his record by talking about his tough schedule, some key injuries, and not inheriting much talent.

"But it didn't take long for him to realize that those little white lies he was telling himself weren't helping. In fact, he said being in denial only delays success. That's when he learned to quit rationalizing the situation and search for the truth. When he finally accepted the truth, he found that his schedule was not any tougher than the other schools' schedules in his district, everyone had injuries, and the talent he inherited was not significantly different than his competitors' talent."

"That's a key point right there," Jeff interjected. "Don't allow yourself to get caught in the excuse trap. Excuses are abundant … and predictable! You will always be able to find one, you'll always find others who will agree with your excuse, and you can rest assured that the excuses will never solve any problem. Two common attributes among successful people are: 1) they do not make excuses to justify why things are the way they are, and 2) they don't complain about the way things should be. They accept reality and take charge to make positive things happen."

I quickly made note of what Jeff was saying and then continued. "Coach Ferguson said he didn't enjoy failing, but failure provided his greatest learning moments because failure taught him humility, perseverance and courage. But most of all, failure taught him to do whatever was necessary to prevent being in the same situation again.

"He made a commitment that From Now On, for every mistake, he would not make the same mistake again. He decided he would study more film, teach better fundamentals, go to every coaching clinic he could, listen more to his assistants, create his game plans around the actual talent on his team, and spend more time giving back to the community."

"Coach Ferguson is a wise man," Jeff acknowledged. "He taught me the same lessons as a high-school athlete. Since that time, I've heard him speak at least a dozen times, and he delivers the same advice – From Now On! I've found that many people are reluctant to learn from the past and move forward. Instead, they're more interested in justifying why the situation is the way it is rather than making the situation better. It's no secret, but success rarely happens on the first try. It usually happens after trial and error, learning from those mistakes, prolonged effort and moving forward."

"I understand," I nodded. "When you say, 'From Now On,' you're really saying, 'Change now!'"

"Exactly!" Jeff replied, "Most people would rather do anything than change ... even when things may not be going well. Do you remember reading a book in high school titled *The Road Less Traveled*?"

"I don't remember that one," I admitted, somewhat embarrassed. "I must have been out of school that day."

"Right," Jeff laughed with me. "Anyway, if you'd been there, you would have learned that the road the author referred to had a sign at the entrance that read, 'Life is difficult.' In fact, those three words were the first page of the book. The reason the road was less traveled was because it was difficult. People would pass it by looking for the road without difficulties – Easy Street.

"Responding to change is like going down the road less traveled. It's not Easy Street but it gets you where you need to be." Jeff continued, "I think one of the reasons I've enjoyed some success is because I like the process of change. I'm not someone who changes just for change's sake, but I enjoy the improvement that comes after a change has been made.

"A lot of people look at me as though I'm crazy when I suggest we change something that is not broken," Jeff said. "Sometimes they don't understand that I'm not trying to break it … I'm just trying to improve so we realize our potential. The way I see it, growth and success are optional, and if we choose that option, we have to change."

"That is a different view," I said. "Most people would say, 'If it's not broken, don't fix it!' In fact, that's what I believe, as well. Why waste time fixing something that's not broken when there are usually plenty of other things that need fixing?"

Jeff thought for a moment, his index finger tracing the rim of his coffee cup. "Believe me, I've heard that point of view many times … and most people agree with you. I even agree that sometimes there are other things that need to be fixed first. But, if you started to fix those things that need fixing, chances are the same people would be opposed to the changes necessary to improve them.

"Change should be constant and welcomed, even when things are going well. Write that down." Jeff gave me a minute to write, then continued. "The late John F. Kennedy once said, 'You fix the roof when the sun is shining,' and there is a lot of wisdom in that statement. You don't wait until the storm to react to something that needs to be fixed.

"Change happens," Jeff said, "so why not decide that From Now On you will welcome it and accept it? I've seen people hunker down and refuse to react to change. Their motto is, 'From Now On I'll keep doing everything exactly as I've been doing it.' Those are the folks who wind up losing everything.

"If you think about it, Ryan, change allows us to move forward and look to the future with confidence. So, in my opinion, the two most important lessons to learn about change are:

1. When change happens ... go with it. Don't sit around waiting and hoping that things will change back to the way they used to be.

2. When things are going well, keep changing. You can only improve if you are making positive changes."

I was intrigued with what Jeff was saying about change. "Maybe I should develop a new habit of welcoming change," I decided.

"I think that would serve you very well," Jeff said. And then he offered one last piece of advice: "Remember, success never comes from just one truth, attitude or phrase. From Now On is an attitude that helps us as we deal with change. Coach Ferguson is a great example of living that truth."

I nodded my agreement. "It seems I've been collecting a Hall of Fame of role models."

"Indeed you have!" Jeff smiled as we stood and walked toward the front door.

"Next week we're going to talk about goals. In the meantime, please call David Cook, a local golf professional. Here's his business card. I've arranged for him to give you a golf lesson at your convenience. I think you'll gather a lot of wisdom from him."

"I don't play golf," I said.

"No problem," Jeff countered. "The lesson you'll get from David will be something you can use in all areas of your life. I promise you'll find it worth your time."

We said our goodbyes, and I got in my car, pulled out my notebook and wrote:

From Now On ...

Key Points:

✔ It's okay to fail – everyone fails at some point – but it's not okay to keep failing.

✔ Denial only delays success.

✔ Success rarely shows up quickly. It appears after trial, error and prolonged effort.

✔ Growth and success are optional, and if we choose that option, we have to change.

✔ Successful people never make excuses to justify why things are the way they are, and they don't complain about the way things should be.

✔ Change should be constant and welcomed, even when things are going well.

✔ Problem-solving process that can be used for virtually any issue – write down:
   1. The problem as you perceive it;
   2. The impact it has on you or others;
   3. What you want to accomplish – your desired end state;
   4. Why you think the problem exists;
   5. Potential solutions.

My Assignment: Learn success truths from David Cook.

Do Something Different:
1. Learn from my mistakes and failures and never make the same mistake twice.
2. Accept reality and take charge to make positive things happen.
3. Welcome change.

The Sixth Tuesday

See It, Feel It, Trust It, Do It!

During the week, I met with David Cook, the golf pro at one of the country clubs in our community. I'd heard he was one of the best teachers in the area ... and maybe in the country. Needless to say, I was a little reluctant to go to such an esteemed pro when I hadn't picked up a golf club in years. But I'd made a commitment at the outset to complete my assignments, so off I went to the golf course. As soon as I met David, however, it became clear that this wasn't going to be your typical golf lesson.

Now, I was really looking forward to sharing David's lesson with Jeff. No sooner had I rung the bell than Jeff opened the door with his usual broad smile. "Come on in, Ryan. I already have the coffee made."

After exchanging a few pleasantries, I asked, "Any news from Mark?"

"Thanks for asking," Jeff replied. "Mark had a really good conversation with his manager. As I suspected, the problem was that they hadn't taken the time to communicate their expectations of each other. Once they put everything on the table, they were able to work through a couple of minor issues. As we talked about before, nothing is ever as bad as it seems ... you just need to be honest with each other and work through issues. The bottom line is that all is fine with Mark and his job."

"Great!" I said. "That's good to hear. I know you were worried about him."

"Yes, I suppose I was," Jeff replied. "Your kids are always your kids no matter how old they are."

Jeff took a sip of coffee and then changed the subject. "So how did your meeting go?"

"I actually enjoyed the golf lesson," I began. "I appreciate you setting that up. It's been a long time since I've had a golf club in my hands, so I was a little nervous when I got there. But, as you probably already know, during the lesson I never actually swung a club. It was the first golf lesson I've ever had where I never even touched a golf club.

"Oh, and here is a sleeve of golf balls David asked me to give to you. He said he hadn't seen you in a while."

"Thanks for the golf balls," Jeff said as he looked them over.

"David knows me well – they are Titleist 8s with 'Simple Truths' imprinted on each ball. I'm sure I'll be putting them to use in the not-too-distant future. It's been a while since I've been able to play, mainly because the weather hasn't cooperated on the days I was available. But it won't be long before I'm back on the links.

"So you took a golf lesson but didn't touch a club?" he repeated, feigning surprise. "How good of a lesson could that be?"

"It was a great lesson," I said. "You didn't tell me that David, the golf pro, was actually David Cook, Ph.D., a sports psychologist."

"I figured you'd find that out soon enough. David has been a friend of mine for a long time," Jeff explained. "So what did you learn?"

"I learned a lot about golf, but the lesson was really a lesson about success," I said. "He taught me the fundamentals of goal setting – seeing what I want to accomplish, feeling the result of the action, trusting that I'm doing the right thing, and then implementing the plan."

"David teaches people how to be successful using golf as a metaphor," Jeff pointed out.

"That's right, and he teaches that the most important part of golf is mental," I continued. "Dr. Cook says the difference between the best golfers and average golfers is in the way they approach the game. He says the typical golfer goes to the range and hits balls for hours, making the same mistakes over and over. On the other hand, the best golfers realize the most important part of golf is what happens between the golfer's ears."

"That's right," Jeff chimed in, once again pleased I'd gotten the point. "Golf is not really a physical game. You can play golf from the time you're 3 years old until the day you're put in your grave. The people who are able to manage the mental part of the game are the ones who enjoy it the most, play the best, and take the most money from their competitors. So, I'm curious. What did Dr. Cook tell you to do?"

"Well, he said before any round, I have to create a plan. The plan may change, based on the wind, temperature, whom I'm playing with, situations that present themselves on the course, or even how I feel on that particular day. His point was that, regardless of circumstances or environment, the game of golf begins in my head.

"The first thing he said I have to do is to establish goals for the round," I said, sensing the same excitement in sharing my experience with Jeff that I'd felt when Dr. Cook had outlined the strategy several days earlier. "Every round begins with me setting specific goals about what I want to accomplish in that round. Since I have no control over what my opponent does, I have to make my goals personal, positive and specific – such as what score I want to shoot, how many putts I'll make during the round, how many greens I'll hit in regulation, etc.

"Dr. Cook explained that the goals have to be measurable as well. So I can't have a goal like 'I want to hit good shots.' How do you measure good shots … or even, what does 'good shot' really mean? My goals must have results, and the goals have to be attainable. If I'm an 18-handicap golfer, my goal for the day should not be to shoot par – that's unrealistic and will only frustrate me and the people I'm playing with.

"The second thing Dr. Cook said was that to be a great golfer, I have to be a great artist."

"Artist?" Jeff questioned. "That's a new one for me."

"Yep. Artist." I explained, "Before I hit a shot, I must visually paint a picture in my mind of what I want the shot to look like. He said my body then will begin to respond to the information it sees in my mind, and my muscles will work off the picture I visualized. So I have to mentally see each shot before I hit it."

"How do you visually paint your shot?" Jeff asked. "In other words, how do you see it?"

"I asked Dr. Cook the same question," I responded, "and he told me to imagine I was playing a hole with water on the left side of the fairway. Then he asked me how I would visualize the shot. I said I'd see the ball landing on the right side of the fairway and wouldn't even visualize the water."

Jeff interrupted, "So, you consciously took the water out of play. Interesting … I think a lot of people focus on the water and how to stay out of it, as opposed to seeing the ball hit perfectly to the other side of the fairway. People tend to focus on the negative or what they don't want to happen, rather than visualizing the positive or what they do want to happen."

"Exactly," I said. "That's the mental exercise he taught me – see the shot where you want it to land. After you see it, then line up your shot and 'feel' the shot, in your mind, hitting your clubface squarely. Once you feel it in your mind, then you have to trust your body and muscles to do the rest.

"Dr. Cook said golf is a game played by memory. You stare at the ball on the ground in front of you before you hit it. Yet you want it to go where you've painted your picture. The painting is the most important part," I related. "Once you see it and can feel it, then trust your swing to take the ball to the spot you painted in your mind. That is David Cook's mental advantage to golf."

"Good stuff, Ryan," Jeff said. "But how does this apply to you? You're not a golfer, so what did you learn from David that will help you be more successful?"

"He explained that everything he'd taught me applies to success and that I could easily transfer it to my life," I answered.

"So goal setting is David's simple truth of success," Jeff pointed out.

"Yes. He said most people who are unhappy in life are unhappy because they don't have goals or a sense of purpose ... kind of like golfers who are unhappy with their golf game are the ones who play golf as a physical rather than mental game.

"Then the lesson really got tough," I confided. "Dr. Cook asked me, 'Do you have clear goals that give purpose to your life? What are your most important goals right now? What steps are you taking to move toward those goals?'

"I sat there and asked myself, *What are my goals?* And the answer was, *I don't know.* Then I realized that if I can't paint a picture of what success looks like to me, how can I feel it and then trust that the activities I'm doing will lead me where I want to go?

"I also realized that I've been more focused on the possibility of failing than on the probability of succeeding. To use David's illustration, I have – up to now – painted my canvas with the 'hazard' dominating the scene … the 'fairway' has barely been in the picture. I've been focusing on my frustrations and have stopped dreaming about what I want to accomplish with my life."

"It sounds like that was a key turning point for you. So, Ryan, are you ready to make some changes From Now On that will make a real difference in your life?"

"You bet," I said, answering almost before Jeff had finished his question. "That's why I'm here."

"Okay, great. As David said, most people don't have specific goals for what they want to accomplish in life, so you're not alone. In fact, you are in the majority. Not having specific goals and keeping our expectations low protect us from disappointment."

"I guess that's supposed to make me feel better?" I wondered out loud.

"Not really. It's just a fact. It is rare for someone to achieve long-term success (in fact, I've never known anyone) when they didn't make deliberate decisions and a conscious effort toward the specific goal they were trying to accomplish. Successful people know exactly what they want … and it is specific, measurable and attainable. You can't see, feel, trust and do something that hasn't been clearly identified.

"When David was teaching you the mental advantage of golf, how many times did you 'create' a shot?"

Jeff's question was puzzling. "I'm not sure exactly what you mean, but let me give it a shot, so to speak. I saw the shot in my mind, felt the shot in my mind, trusted the shot when I looked at the ball, and then – if I'd had a club in my hand – I would have hit it. I'd say about four times."

"Right! Your personal and professional goals are exactly the same ... you 'create' them four times. First, you see the goal as a mental picture, then you feel it when you write the goal down, then you trust it when you tell others, and finally you do it when you take action toward the goal. It's the same four steps that David taught you about your golf shot. See, feel, trust and do."

"Is it really necessary to go through each of those steps?" I asked. "For example, why do I have to write my goals down or tell someone else what they are?"

"It's critical for you to follow all four steps," Jeff explained. "Think about it ... would David's mental advantage for golf work if you didn't go through all four steps? No. It's like a recipe – if you leave out a step or an ingredient, you're not going to get the same result."

"You write your goals down because writing clarifies your thoughts – there is power in writing. Sometimes it's hard to 'see' our goals vividly in our mind, but it's difficult to be vague when you write thoughts on paper. Writing clarifies the situation and helps you answer the questions: *Is the goal worthwhile?* and *Is this goal attainable?* If the answer is 'no' to either of these reality questions, you need to re-think your goal.

"And the reason it's important to tell others is that it holds you accountable to someone and helps you move forward ... and, hopefully, you can bring someone on the trip with you.

"Here is how I use David's four-step process to set my goals," Jeff said as he handed me a piece of paper outlining the goal-setting process:

1. See It!

Envision the goal in your mind. Visualize it as a positive situation – what you want to happen (ball on the fairway) rather than what you don't want to happen (ball in the water).

2. Feel It!

✦ Write the goal on paper and describe it in positive, personal and present tense. (For example: I am a non-smoker on June 18.)

✦ Do a "reality check" and attach emotion to the goal by asking these questions:

- *Why do I want to achieve this goal?* (For example: better health, save money, family desire, etc.)

- *Is this goal intensely desired?*

- *Is it achievable and realistic?*

- *Am I willing to pay the price to achieve the goal?*

3. TRUST IT!

Who can you tell that will support you and hold you accountable?

4. DO IT!

Every minute spent in planning will save you five minutes in execution. Make a plan to accomplish your goal, including:

- ✦ Where are you starting from/what is your current situation? (For example: I currently smoke two packs a day.)

- ✦ Set a deadline/date to accomplish the goal. (Example: By June 18, I will achieve this goal.)

- ✦ Identify the obstacles to overcome. (Example: I have a habit of smoking when I am in my car.)

- ✦ Determine whose help you will need to accomplish the goal.

- ✦ How are you going to accomplish the goal? Specifically list the activities required as well as the priority of activities.

"That's a lot of work," I acknowledged. "The process is more involved than I've ever used before. As I told you a couple of weeks ago, the most difficult thing for me is understanding, exactly and specifically, what I really want. I believe the step of writing the goal down will help me paint my canvas more vividly. Then I think the other steps will come relatively easy."

Jeff agreed. "I assure you they will. You're absolutely right when you say the most difficult thing is to clearly understand what you want ... but it's also the most important thing.

"The same process applies in all areas of your life. The most successful people I know have specific goals for their body, mind and soul ... and I believe each of those areas are interdependent and affect all the other areas of your life. Your work will be better if you have a healthy body, a compassionate soul and you feed your mind with new and positive ideas. If you focus on improving each of those areas, you'll discover that they all get stronger together."

"So are you saying I need goals in all areas of my life?" I asked. "That is certainly a lot of stuff going on at once."

"Yes, Ryan," Jeff said, "and that requires discipline."

"Discipline is not a real positive word for me," I confessed. "But I remember hearing someone say, 'We all must suffer from two pains: the pain of discipline or the pain of regret.' Right now, I'll be the first to admit, I'm on the regret side of pain."

"I understand," Jeff said, "and the good news is that it's never too late to participate in the pain of discipline. As you and I both know, success does not come easily. If you want easy, you'll never achieve success. The valuable things in life are hard to get, which is why so many people do not even have goals in their lives.

"To be successful, you have to work as hard on yourself as you do in your job," he continued. "As I said, all the areas of your life are interdependent. You will not achieve success if you lose your family, health or compassion. And it's also important to remember that success is not measured by money – you will never have the most money. Success is measured by the lives you positively affect."

At this point, Jeff looked at his watch and saw that our time was coming to an end. "The last point I want to make on goal-setting is to pay close attention to the people you're spending time with. My friend, Billy Cox, says, 'You will become like the five people you spend the most time with' ... and that can be a blessing or a curse," he added. "You need to be around people who bless you, not curse you, and that is a decision you control."

"But a lot of the time, the people I'm with is out of my control," I said in my own defense. "As you know, I deal with customers, employees and even some family members and friends who are not blessings to me."

"Yes, you have to tolerate them, Ryan, but you can choose not to allow them to pull you down," Jeff warned. "You can choose to not accept their negativity and cynicism.

"You control your actions," he went on to explain. "If you want to attract positive people, you must act positive. To attract committed people, you must act committed. To attract successful people, you must act successful. Who you become is who you will attract. If you want to be a positive, committed, successful person, you must see it, feel it, trust it, and do it," he concluded.

"So, Ryan, what are you going to do differently based on this week's lesson?" Jeff wanted to know.

"First, I'm going to set some goals now that I have a definitive process to follow," I began. "Second, I'm going to watch what and who I am attracting. I think I've been responsible for allowing myself to be around people who were pulling me down instead of lifting me up. Third, I'm going to take the first step toward learning how to play golf. It seems to me there are a lot of life lessons that can be learned on the golf course."

"Just what I wanted to hear," Jeff smiled. "Next week I want to talk about how you can get more done in less time. So your assignment for this week is to read this book."

I read the title of the small book he'd handed me: "*Time! 105 Ways to Get More Done Every Workday.* Great! I certainly need to learn how to manage my time better. I'll read it and see you next week."

When I got into my car, I wrote in my notebook:

See It, Feel It, Trust It, Do It

Key Points:

✔ I've been more focused on the possibility of failing than I have on succeeding — that has to change now!

✔ I can't see, feel, trust and do something that has not been clearly and specifically identified.

✔ If I want easy, I will not achieve success.

✔ I will become like the five people I spend the most time with...and that can be a blessing or a curse.

✔ To attract successful people, I must act successful

My Assignment: Read Time! 105 Ways to Get More Done Every Workday

Do Something Different:

1. Set goals using the four-step See It, Feel It, Trust It, Do It process.

2. Act in a manner consistent with whom and what I want to attract.

The Seventh Tuesday

Focus Inside Your Boat

Jeff was excited when he greeted me at the door for our seventh meeting. "Did you see the Olympics last night? Man, did our team hand it to the Canadian hockey team or what? Could you believe that game?"

I had no idea Jeff was a hockey fan, but he lit up as he recounted the big upset. "I didn't see it," I confessed, "but I heard about it. Must have been a great game."

"Great game?" Jeff shouted. "It was unbelievable! Unfortunately, I bet we'll have to face them again in the finals. I just hope we have what it takes to beat them again. Anyway, I've been watching the Olympics as long as I can remember. Matter of fact, I'm a big fan of both the Winter and Summer games … and that game was one of the most exciting events I've seen."

"I love the Olympics, too, but I just haven't been able to find the time to watch much of the games this year," I admitted.

"Well, whether you know it or not, Ryan, not having time for things you enjoy is your choice. If you stop and think about it, you have as much time as anyone else. So maybe you need to figure out how to use your time better so you can enjoy some of the pleasures of life. In my opinion, if you want something bad enough, you will make the time to do it. You always have enough time for the things that are important to you if you spend it right."

"I definitely need to work on my time management," I agreed with Jeff. "But before we get started, I've got something else to tell you. I used your goal-setting process this week. It was just a small goal, but I went through the process, step by step … and it works! It added substance to a plan that would have resided only in my head.

"I thought through every step, involved other people in the process and now – get this – I'm going to teach the process to my team. I think it will make a huge difference in how we get things done."

"Terrific," Jeff said. "I'm living proof that having a goal-setting process is one of the keys to success. The process that seems so cumbersome the first few times you go through it will become almost automatic, the more you use it. Becoming a goal-setting expert will pay big dividends for you. Guaranteed.

"Now … back to your time management," Jeff redirected. "I remember when we talked the first week you came, you commented that life was slipping by. Maybe there are some things you can do to get control back. That's what I'd like to talk about today … taking control of your time and your life. Did you read the book I gave you last week?"

That was the question I'd been dreading. "Actually …," I said hesitantly, "I didn't. I started to read it yesterday at lunch and was going to finish it last night. When I packed up my things at the end of the day, I couldn't find it. I realized I must have left it in the break room, but when I went back to get it, it was gone. All the local bookstores were sold out of it, and there wasn't time to order one online. I realize this means that I haven't lived up to the commitment I made our first week to complete my assignments. Honestly, I was looking forward to reading it … especially because time management is a subject I certainly could use some help with."

Jeff became very serious. "You're right. You haven't lived up to your commitment. I thought I could Consider It Done when I gave you that assignment."

"I know … believe me, I know. I've been stressed about it ever since. But it wasn't like I forgot … I did try to complete the assignment," I said a bit defensively.

"Yes, but the bottom line is that you didn't," Jeff said.

"I guess I shouldn't have put it off until the last day," I offered. "I'm sorry."

"Apology accepted." Jeff's tone lightened some. "Well, the upside is – and there's always an upside to every situation – that your procrastination dovetails perfectly with what we're going to talk about today.

"Here's another copy of the book," Jeff said, taking another little book from a nearby shelf. "I keep several of these books on hand to give to friends. I find that managing priorities is a challenge for everyone. I hope whoever took your book will read it ... and I hope you'll take the time to read it soon yourself."

Jeff settled back in his chair and balanced his fingertips together in front of him. "Ryan, do you remember a sportscaster named Charlie Jones? He may have been before your time, but he was a legendary sportscaster who covered several Olympic Games."

I told Jeff that I once knew a Charlie Jones, but I'd never heard of a sportscaster by that name.

"No harm," he said, "but you would have loved listening to Charlie. He was a great broadcaster. I remember a story he told on television that made an impact on me. At the 1996 games in Atlanta, Charlie was assigned to announce the rowing, canoeing and kayaking events – a situation that left him less than thrilled since he was a prime-time broadcaster and these events were to be taped at 7:00 in the morning. On top of that, the water venue was an hour drive from Atlanta.

"What Charlie discovered, however, was that covering those less popular competitions ended up being some of the most memorable sporting events of his career. He said that he had the chance to understand the mental workings of those Olympic athletes ... athletes he knew virtually nothing about.

"Charlie explained that to prepare for the broadcast, he interviewed several of the rowers. He asked them what they would do in case of rain, strong winds or choppy water. The response was always the same: 'That's outside my boat.' After hearing the same answer again and again, Charlie realized these Olympic athletes had a remarkable focus. They were interested only in what they could control ... and that was what was happening inside their boat. Everything else was beyond their control and not worth expending the mental energy and attention that would distract them from their ultimate task.

"If you think about it, that's a pretty good lesson for all of us, not just Olympic athletes," Jeff said. "Keep focused on what is 'inside your boat,' because that is the only thing you can control. Of course, that's easier said than done."

"I like that ... that makes a lot of sense to me," I said as I jotted down some notes.

"Me too," Jeff agreed. "We all have moments when we need to redirect our efforts 'inside our boat' to keep ourselves focused on what's important. We have to use our time, energy, attention and efforts on the things we can control.

"Now that we are talking about our time and focus, do you think you can manage time?" Jeff asked.

"Absolutely!" I asserted. "I've been told almost all my life that I needed to learn how to manage my time better."

"That's interesting. How do you manage time?" Jeff asked and then kept talking. "It's my guess no one explained that ... and for good reason: Time is not manageable. No matter what you do, time marches on at its own pace – tick, tick, tick – and there's nothing you can do to change that.

"Time is a great equalizer. It runs at the same speed for everybody, rich or poor, jet pilot or snail farmer. True, time seems to run faster when you're out with friends, slower when you're sitting in the doctor's waiting room, but it's actually chugging along at a constant pace – exactly 168 hours a week – leaving behind a trail of unrecoverable seconds, minutes and hours.

"Have you ever attended a time management class?" Jeff asked.

"While I was working with you, in fact, I participated in a time management class at the company," I answered.

Jeff nodded, saying he recalled several held during his tenure with the corporation. "That was a while back, but do you recall what you learned?" he asked.

"The only thing I remember is that I needed to make a to-do list. Initially, I was pretty faithful about making that list, but recently, I seem to have gotten out of that habit."

"To-do lists are fine," Jeff interjected. "Making lists and checking things off the list can be useful, even satisfying. It's great to experience that 'rush' of accomplishment we get when we check something off. However, most people discover at the end of the day, week or month, there are still projects that are not checked off and some projects they haven't even started. That's when frustration begins to set in. The time is gone, and there's no way to get it back. You can't manufacture time. You can't reproduce time. You can't slow time down or turn it around and make it run in the other direction. You can't trade bad hours for good ones, either."

Jeff was on a roll. "What you can manage, however, is your attention. It's inside your boat – something you can control," he explained. "Attention is a resource we all possess. In fact, as long as we are awake, we produce a continuous stream of it. But how effectively do we use this valuable resource? That depends on where we direct our attention and how intensely we keep it focused on what we are trying to accomplish.

"Your attention reflects your conscious decisions about which activities will occupy your time," Jeff pointed out. "One of the challenges we face in managing our attention is that today's world is connected. We are connected to more potential time robbers than ever before.

"Speaking of being connected, do you use any of the social sites on the Web?"

"Pretty much all of them at one time or another," I replied.

"So you're probably LinkedIn, Facebooked and MySpaced, right? You're being pinged, Tweeted, IMed, e-mailed, blogged and Blackberried or iPhoned. You may be LexisNexised, Yahooed and Googled with real-time news alerts, stock updates and traffic reports. I suspect Earth-orbiting satellites know where you are every second, how many inches you are from your favorite restaurant and whether your air bags have deployed. You're probably so connected, you've forgotten what it's like to be alone with your own thoughts."

"I can certainly relate to that," I laughed, impressed that he knew all the modern technology available.

"Your job probably involves multiple responsibilities that are constantly pulling your attention in many different directions," Jeff continued. "You have the ability to recognize when things need to be done and direct your attention to doing them. So the question becomes: Why do we so often run out of time before getting the important things done?"

"Things happen," I rationalized. "Sometimes I go home after working hard all day and can't tell Michele one specific thing I accomplished that day."

"That's because you let your attention get diverted by things outside your boat," Jeff explained. "There's usually a plausible reason – an unexpected event or other distraction that seemed important at the time. You may even be able to justify why you couldn't get your important tasks done. Or maybe you just weren't firing on all eight cylinders that day.

"But here's the deal: The problem is not time ... and it's not your to-do list. You knew how much time you had that day, and you made out a list of what you wanted to do with that time. The problem is, your attention was reallocated to something that didn't lead you toward your goals."

"So, if I can't manage my time ... how can I start managing my attention?" I asked.

"Good question. In a nutshell, the most successful people are really good at three things:

    1. Identifying their priorities;

2. Knowing when to say 'no;' and

3. Attacking procrastination.

"The first step to managing your attention is to precisely understand your priorities," Jeff said. "There's a big difference between managing your attention to accomplish priorities and checking off items on your to-do list.

"Our natural tendency is to do what is fun, convenient or absolutely necessary at any given time. But your true priorities may not fit into any of those categories," he explained. "In the absence of clearly defined goals, you'll find yourself involved in trivial pursuits … pursuits that will keep you from doing what needs to be done to accomplish those goals. You'll somehow convince yourself that you're accomplishing something."

"I can relate to that!" I confessed, thinking about some of the easy things I do instead of the important things I need to be doing.

"It's a bad idea to try to fool yourself about how productively you're managing your attention," Jeff said. "Here's something to ask yourself to help you stay on track: *If I could accomplish only one thing right now, what would that one thing be?* Your answer will quickly identify what your priority should be and where you should be directing your attention. Write that priority at the top of your to-do list and move everything else down – or completely off – the list."

"What about when I have multiple priorities at once? Can I multitask to get them done at the same time?" I inquired.

"Ryan, you can multitask only if you want to do multiple

things poorly. Even back in the early part of the 20th century, Henry Ford believed that a weakness of all human beings was trying to do too many things at once. 'That scatters effort and destroys direction,' Ford is noted as saying. 'Every now and then I wake up in the morning with a dozen things I want to do. I know I can't do them all at once.' When asked what he did about that, Ford replied, 'I go out and trot around the house. While I'm running off the excess energy that wants to do too much, my mind clears and I see what can be done and should be done first.'

"You have to set your goals, identify your priorities and manage your attention toward those priorities," Jeff emphasized. "And as you identify priorities, be realistic about what you can accomplish. It's your job to know exactly where and how to invest your attention.

"Although important tasks that relate to your goals are your top priorities, most of the time, these are not the things that appear to be urgent," he continued. "Don't be fooled into thinking that whatever seems urgent is worth taking your mind off your most important goals. President Eisenhower's mantra during his regime was 'What's important is seldom urgent, and what's urgent is seldom important.'"

"I hear you," I chimed in. "I think I'm like most people who prioritize the easy, fun stuff and postpone the more difficult tasks, even when they are the most important things."

"Right you are, and you're definitely not alone there," Jeff said.

"The second area you need to address with respect to attention management is understanding when to say 'no,'" he continued. "Here's a trick question: Which is more powerful – the sun or a laser beam?"

"Well, since it's a trick question, I'd say the laser beam," I said. "Although I would have said the sun since it gives light to everything, including the laser."

"Good job! You're correct on both fronts. The sun puts out 600 billion kilowatts of energy. Yet you can deflect most of its harmful effects with a thin application of sunscreen. On the other hand, a laser beam focusing only a few kilowatts of energy can cut a diamond in half and eradicate certain types of cancer.

"Laser-like clarity about what is important should be your objective, Ryan. One of the most important decisions you can make is to decide what's most important. As you already know, your time and energy are precious resources. Once you spend them, you don't get them back. Therefore, saying 'yes' to one thing always means saying 'no' to something else. Successful people create laser-like focus by saying 'no' to low-priority activities so they can say 'yes' to the things they are really committed to – their top goals and priorities.

"It's hard to say 'no' to others," Ryan interjected. "Most of the time, they're asking for something that is important to them.

"Hold on," Jeff said. "Don't think saying 'no' just means saying it to others. Most of the time, successful people say 'no' to themselves. They sacrifice the comforts of today – by saying 'no' to something that might be fun or tempting – so they can gain tomorrow's rewards. They are really saying 'yes' to their ultimate goal.

"Saying 'no' is not a once-in-a-while thing, either. Instead, it's a daily, winning habit. For example, if you spend two hours in a meeting that doesn't help your team achieve its goals, you're paying an opportunity cost by spending time on tasks that do not support your commitments. If you find yourself frequently saying, 'That was a waste of time,' or 'Boy, that didn't add any value,' or 'Why was I attending that meeting?' – these questions may be signs you need to start saying 'no.'

"The best attention management question you can ask yourself is: 'Is this the best use of my attention at this moment?' If it is, then get busy. If not, then refocus.

"When planning your goals, in addition to the things you need to do to achieve the goals, create a 'stop-doing' list as well. Write down all activities, tasks, reports, meetings, and projects that do not directly support your goals. This will help you focus your attention more effectively on the things that are most important to you – whether it's at work, at home or in the community.

"So why do you think we find ourselves saying 'yes' when we should be saying 'no'?" Jeff asked.

"Probably because we're afraid we'll hurt someone's feelings and damage our relationship," I said after thinking about Jeff's question a few moments.

"I understand," Jeff said, "but I don't agree. Here's why: You have no control over another person's feelings. Again, that's outside your boat. If you're honest in telling someone what your priorities are and why you have to say 'no,' most of the time they will respect that. In my opinion, they would rather hear, 'Sorry, I can't do it' up front than 'I'm sorry, I didn't get to it' later.

"Just tell the truth. If saying 'no' could damage the relationship, your relationship is probably pretty toxic already. Relationships are damaged more by misunderstandings and unspoken perceptions than by disagreements," he continued. "If you are open and honest, chances are you'll be able to work through an issue of disagreement."

"But what about my boss or the people I work with?" I asked. "Sometimes I can't say 'no' to them."

"You are ultimately responsible for achieving results," Jeff said. "If it's clear that the activity your supervisor or team members is suggesting will keep you from accomplishing your priorities, you need to say 'no' and be clear about why you are saying 'no.' If you explain your priorities and they're not in line with the priorities of your boss or team members, something is out of sync.

"Ryan, there is great power in understanding your goals and priorities and maintaining a laser-like focus. Effectively managing your attention boils down to self-discipline," Jeff explained. "There is no set formula. What works for someone else may not work for you because your priorities are different. However, if you know your priorities, focus your attention and consistently make the best use of your attention, you'll discover the right things will get done."

I needed to gather my thoughts before Jeff took off in another direction. "So let me summarize: I need to focus inside my boat – on the things I can control. I need to know my priorities with laser-like clarity and be honest with those who try to divert me from my priorities."

"That's about it," Jeff said. "Makes sense, doesn't it?"

"It does make sense," I agreed. "Now that I've set my goals, it will be much easier to identify my priorities."

"Absolutely!" Jeff concurred. "Now, let's take on the third area of attention management – procrastination."

I stopped writing long enough to joke, "Why don't we put that off until next week, Jeff?"

"Very funny – I didn't realize you were a comedian," he laughed. "At least you were listening. Now, why do you think attacking procrastination is important?"

"I guess because when something goes undone, it sort of hangs over my head and is always on my mind ... almost like a distraction."

"That's exactly the way I feel as well," Jeff agreed. "One of the most important simple truths to learn is to 'Do it Now!' That's the key to dealing with procrastination. In almost every situation, procrastination is an enemy – a nasty habit that can cost you a lot of time, energy and frustration.

"Putting things off seldom improves the quality of your work," he continued. "In fact, like you said, knowing you have something to do that should already be done just increases stress. So to stop procrastination, you have to have your laser-focus on your priorities. Sound familiar?"

"Déjà vu," I answered. "Crystal-clear focus on what is important. I said that was the hardest part of attention management for me."

"That's why I keep emphasizing it," Jeff responded. "You have to recognize and admit that procrastination is stealing your time, adding stress to your life, and keeping you from your priorities. You have to consciously attack procrastination by having the mindset that there is no better time to get things done, so Do It Now!

"If there's a task you especially dislike and it's a priority, do it first ... and then, as if by magic, it goes away!" Jeff smiled. "And make sure to reward yourself every time you complete a task you wanted to delay. This will give you incentive to knock out other unpleasant tasks as they come along.

"Do It Now also means to be decisive," Jeff continued. "When someone says to you, 'Call me later and we'll set an appointment,' respond by saying, 'Let's save ourselves a call and make the appointment now.' Then it's done, and you won't have to spend another 15 minutes on a phone call just to arrange a meeting. It also seems a lot more sincere, doesn't it? 'Call me later' is some people's polite way of saying, 'I don't really care that much about it.'

"Ryan, the bottom line is that you can do better. You can identify your priorities, know when to say 'no,' and Do It Now to attack procrastination," Jeff concluded.

"What about Do It Now if you don't have all the facts? Wouldn't that create more work in the long run?" I wondered.

"Procrastination doesn't begin until you have all the facts needed to move forward," Jeff clarified.

"Here is one last Do It Now suggestion: Clear your inbox every day. That important e-mail that came the other day – or was it last week – that you didn't answer? Well, now it's nagging at you. You've wasted 15 minutes just looking for it and still can't find it. You can only hope it wasn't a crisis with a customer or supplier."

"Been there, done that," I admitted.

"Take control by developing an 'in-today, out-tomorrow' process for all e-mails and paper mail coming into your office. Don't let your inbox pile up. Act on it immediately – Do It Now. Don't worry. I guarantee you – more will show up tomorrow!"

Jeff glanced at his watch. "Looks like we're out of time for today. Now, by my calculation, we have one meeting remaining. Our final lesson will be about firefighting."

"Firefighting?" I asked.

"Yes, firefighting. So before our meeting next Tuesday, I want you to visit one last person – our local fire chief, Ralph Hendricks. Like the others you've met, Chief Hendricks is expecting your call. Set a time to meet with him. You may be surprised to discover what our firefighters can teach us about success."

After wrapping up our session, I wrote in my notebook:

Focus Inside Your Boat

Key Points:

✔ I can't manage time, but I can manage my attention.

✔ I have to precisely identify my priorities.

✔ Successful people say "no" to low-priority activities so they can say "yes" to the things they are really committed to — their top goals and priorities.

✔ Multitask only if you want to do multiple things poorly.

✔ Do It Now to attack procrastination.

My Assignment: Learn success truths from Ralph Hendricks.

Do Something Different:

1. Focus inside my boat...on the things I can control.

2. Create a laser-like focus on my priorities by asking, "If I could accomplish only one thing right now, what would that one thing be?"

3. Manage my attention by asking, "Is this the best use of my attention at this moment?"

The Eighth Tuesday

Knowledge Is Power

I arrived at Jeff's house for our final coaching session on a rainy, chilly Tuesday morning. Despite the weather, I could immediately sense Jeff's enthusiasm, and I wondered what was going on.

"Hey, Ryan," Jeff bellowed as he opened the door. "Today is graduation day! Glad you made it on time. I could hardly wait for you to get here so I could hear about your visit with Ralph. I make it a point of visiting his station frequently because I've learned so much from him and his firefighting team over the years."

We filled our cups with steaming coffee and made our way to the library.

"Before I fill you in on my meeting with Ralph," I said, settling into my chair in the library, "I want to tell you that the book you gave me – *Time! 105 Ways to Get More Done Every Workday* – is terrific. I noticed you covered many of the concepts in our meeting last week, but it was an easy read and I picked up several more tips I could use right away. Thanks for the book – twice," I said, somewhat embarrassed about my earlier procrastination that caused me to lose the first book.

"I'm glad you found it valuable," Jeff said. "So what about Ralph? Did you enjoy meeting our fire chief?"

"I must admit that I wasn't very enthused about visiting with the fire chief," I said. "I didn't think we had anything in common and wasn't sure I could learn anything from his operation. Truthfully, Jeff, I thought I might spend 20 minutes or so with him. I guess that's because my perception was that firefighters spend their time drinking coffee, playing dominos and just waiting around for something to happen. Man, was I wrong! I spent over three hours with Ralph, and every minute was a learning experience."

Jeff seemed pleased. "I knew you would get a lot out of it. I'm eager to hear what you learned."

"Well, first of all, the firefighters are the best-trained team I've ever seen," I said. "They train every day to prepare for virtually any kind of emergency that could arise.

"Ralph's success truth is 'Knowledge Is Power.' He believes that if his people know the fundamentals of fire and understand fire behavior, they will be prepared and the fire will not surprise them. So learning and training is a huge part of everything they do.

"He explained that the objective of firefighting is always the same – put the fire out and return home safely," I continued. "But the methods of firefighting change with the conditions. Most firefighters will not see the same exact fire twice in their careers. That's why they must have tremendous knowledge and be prepared for the situations that present themselves every day. 'In firefighting – just as in business and life – how we prepare counts,'" I said, repeating what Ralph had told me.

"Ralph teaches his team that every fire is different, based on its location, the type of materials that are burning, and the weather. He shows them how to read smoke so they will understand how a fire is burning. They must learn precisely how much water pressure they need to use in order to extinguish a fire without the hose becoming overly stiff and difficult to move."

Checking my notes, I added, "Knowledge is particularly crucial for firefighters since much of their work is done with limited vision due to dense smoke. They depend on each other to communicate the situation and to be where they are supposed to be. Every member of the team at the fire is accountable for completion of his assignment. To fail in any area could be disastrous.

"Ralph believes Knowledge Is Power because knowledge saves lives. It's as simple as that," I explained. "He said that knowledge gives you the power to choose. Firefighters have to know what their options are and what they are going to do if things go wrong. And, they have to understand when it's time to fight and when it's time to get out – and be able to make that decision without hesitation. That comes from knowledge and preparation. And because they are so well trained, their instincts take over in a crisis."

"I knew you would enjoy talking to the chief," Jeff said. "And, as you know, our firefighters are special people who put everything on the line."

"You know, it was interesting," I said. "Ralph also told me that to be a great firefighter, you have to be lucky sometimes … and that a lot of people are confused about luck. He said that most people think that luck seeks them out, when actually the opposite is true – you create luck by increasing your knowledge and being prepared. So the more you learn, the better your decisions … and the luckier you will be."

Jeff nodded and smiled. "I was hoping you'd hear Ralph's philosophy about luck."

"I'll tell you, Jeff, I learned a lot from Ralph during the time we spent together."

"So now, Ryan, tell me how can you implement some of the things you learned from Ralph."

"Well, first, I'm now convinced that Knowledge Is Power, no matter what profession you're in," I responded. "And I know I have to make some changes, like increasing my knowledge on a daily basis."

"Sounds good so far," Jeff said. "What else?"

I had to swallow a lot of ego to answer, but I was ready. "Until we began our Tuesday morning coaching sessions, I wasn't fully aware of the knowledge available to me," I said. "You have given me some tremendous insights during our sessions. When we started, I thought real success was available to only a few. I had convinced myself that success was a series of strategic events – coupled with some luck, of course.

"But, Jeff, you taught me that success can be created by defining and living by some simple truths ... truths that, individually, may not help much, but when put together, they become powerful. And these simple truths are available to everyone."

Jeff seemed pleased. "Absolutely! You probably didn't expect to learn from a coach, cab driver, fire chief, receptionist, or golf pro. But through this experience, you've realized the key to success is to keep learning and increasing your knowledge. No matter what you want to accomplish, you will need more knowledge than you have now. When someone is headed down the wrong path, a lot of people will try to motivate them, which only speeds up their arrival at the wrong place. What they need is knowledge so they can turn themselves around and get back on the right track.

"Many people assume their education was complete when they graduated," Jeff continued. "Actually, the day you graduate is the day your education really begins. What separates the most successful people from others is their quest to continually learn.

"So do you think it's a coincidence that, in most cases, the bigger the house, the bigger the library inside the house?"

Jeff asked rhetorically. "Check it out the next time you visit someone's home. See what kind of books they have on their bookshelves. Believe it or not, you can tell a lot about a person by the books they read. Show me their library, and that library will show me the owner's philosophy and values."

I marveled to myself. Jeff's philosophies were so simple, it could be easy to miss some of the richness of the lessons. I was glad for his coaching.

Jeff continued, "If you are searching for just one activity that provides a great ROI (Return on Investment), read books. Check this out: According to the U.S. Labor Department, business people who read at least seven business books per year earn over 230 percent more than people who read just one book per year. Can you believe that? 230 percent – that's astounding!"

He stopped long enough to let me catch up with my note-taking. "Now here's a question for you: How many books a year do you think the CEOs of major organizations read?"

I scratched my head. Was this another trick question? "I have no idea," I answered finally. "I guess a book a month or so. That's probably all they have time for."

Jeff was intense. "On average, CEOs of major organizations are said to read four books a month. Yet most of the people working for them do not read four books in a lifetime. Does that make sense?"

Without thinking, I said, "Four books a month? That sounds like an exaggeration to me. Who has that amount of time to read?"

Jeff jumped in. "It's probably not an exaggeration, Ryan. Think about it – their primary job is to have and create knowledge. That's a major priority for any leader.

"A lot of people say they don't have time to read," he continued. "That's simply not true. How many books do you think you would have to read to be in the top 1 percent of all non-fiction readers in the world?"

"I would guess a couple, maybe three, books a month," I said lamely.

"Good guess, but actually, you can be in the top 1 percent by reading just one book per month. One book per month is about half a chapter a day, maybe 10 minutes. Top 1 percent for 10 minutes a day investment? What a deal! Think about it. If you read one book a month for one year, you would have read 12 books. In five years, you would have read 60! If you'd read 60 books and you went to interview for a job, don't you think you'd be more knowledgeable than any other candidate for that job?" he asked.

"I would think so."

"Of course you would," said Jeff, obviously passionate about the subject. "The challenge is not finding the time. The challenge is being disciplined and making the pursuit of knowledge a habit and a priority in your life.

"Think about when you asked the others what led to their success. Did your knowledge increase? Was your thinking challenged? Were you surprised at some of the answers?"

"My thinking has definitely changed," I confessed. "And I was surprised to learn that, regardless of one's chosen profession, the truths for success are basically the same. I've learned that success can be achieved by doing a lot of simple things well. Each person you sent me to see taught me that success was not something that happened to them due to luck or even their unique talents. Success was achieved because of their desire and determination to make it happen. They worked hard but enjoyed the trip because they had a positive mission.

"And, I also learned that I do what I prioritize. In the past, I had not made discipline, goal setting, accepting responsibility or any of our other lessons a priority. I was just coasting along. When we began our meetings, I made it a priority to be here on time and ready to learn every Tuesday at 7:00," I said. "If we had not met and I had not been exposed to your knowledge, I would have spent the same time doing something else that would not have impacted my life like our meetings. I would have been just as busy but not getting anywhere. That is how I got into my rut in the first place."

Now it was Jeff's turn. "I can assure you, I have gotten as much out of our lessons as you have because I was preparing for each session," he said. "Our sessions have been a positive push for me to grow and learn. You see, the best way to increase knowledge is to teach someone else. You've provided me the opportunity to increase my knowledge, as well," he added.

"I understand," I replied. "You were giving your knowledge away ... and the more you give, the more you get, right?"

"Absolutely correct," Jeff agreed. "The more you give, the more you get. But that's not why you should give. You shouldn't give just so you can get something back. You give so you will have more to give. I gave my knowledge to you and now I have more knowledge to give to someone else. See, you give more so that you will have more to give.

"Now, here we are at the end of our Tuesday Morning Coaching sessions. One last time, Ryan, I'll ask you, 'What are you going to do differently?'"

I handed a sheet of paper to Jeff. "I knew you would ask that question. Here is my plan."

Ryan Harris' Success Plan

No Matter What – I accept responsibility and move forward.

And Then Some – I give what is expected and then some.

·Consider It Done – I am consistent and dependable.

Above All Else – I adhere to my values.

From Now On – I learn from my mistakes and welcome change.

See It, Feel It, Trust I, Do It – I am a champion goal-setter.

Focus Inside the Boat – I manage my attention and defeat procrastination.

"And after today's session, I'm going to add: Knowledge Is Power – I am a lifelong learner.

"I've created goals in each of those areas that are specific, measurable and achievable," I explained. "These lessons have changed not only how I think but also my perspective on life, as well."

"Wonderful, Ryan! We have come a long way together over the past eight weeks. You are much closer to reaching your goals now because you have more knowledge. And you have discovered one more truth: The more you learn, the more you earn. The more knowledge you have, the more respect, freedom, happiness and success you will earn! You become more valuable to everyone. And, as you well know, people search out those who have learned the most."

Jeff was quiet after this last statement. Then he spoke: "Ryan, why do you think I asked you to go see all of those people?"

"Because," I said, "they are doing what I am trying to do – live a life of success. What was ironic to me is that none of them have the same job that I have, yet all of them have helped me. Each person made the conscious decision to live their life by making better choices rather than depending on luck to get them where they wanted to go. Being lucky will never provide me with the knowledge I need to be successful," I concluded. "I have to pursue knowledge – and then take my chances."

"Exactly!" Jeff beamed. "They had the knowledge you were seeking – and Knowledge Is Power. And the beauty of knowledge is that it is readily available. You don't have to leave your desk to learn. For example, the book I was reading when you arrived for our first visit is available to you or anyone else. You could even borrow it for free from the library. Knowledge is everywhere, but it will not come looking for you ... you have to search for it.

"Speaking of knowledge," Jeff continued. "You have one final assignment."

"Assignment?" I asked. "But isn't this our last session?"

"Yes, it is. But do you remember when you first contacted me several months ago to ask for my help? I agreed to coach you if you would agree to coach others."

"I remember," I said.

"That is your final – and ongoing – assignment," Jeff explained. "To share with others the simple truths you've learned over these last eight weeks."

"I have to admit that I didn't fully understand what I was committing to back then. But now I get it … I need to pay it forward, so to speak," I said. "That is something I can definitely do and an assignment I will thoroughly enjoy. I've learned so much from you and the others – I'm anxious to share it!

"Before we wrap things up, I have something for you," I said as I opened my briefcase. I presented Jeff with a gift of four coffee mugs inscribed with some of the simple truths he had shared with me. "Jeff, I will never be able to repay you for your time and knowledge, but here is a token of my appreciation."

"Thank you," Jeff said. "These are wonderful – they will help me remember and practice the eight simple truths."

As I walked through his door for the last time, I looked back and thanked Jeff again.

"The pleasure was mine," Jeff said. "Just remember: Teach what you know to others."

"I will, Jeff," I promised. "I will."

When I reached my car, I wrote in my notebook:

Knowledge Is Power

Key Points:

✔ The truths for success are basically the same, regardless of the profession.

✔ Knowledge will not come looking for me. I have to seek it out.

✔ What separates the most successful people from others is their quest to continually learn.

✔ If you are searching for just one activity that provides a great ROI, read books.

✔ The more I learn, the more success I will earn.

My Assignment: Teach others the eight simple truths I've learned.

Do Something Different:

1. Develop a daily habit of increasing knowledge.

2. Create "luck" by increasing knowledge and being prepared.

3. Give so I have the opportunity to give more.

Epilogue

Not too long ago while touring Boston, I passed a cemetery where Ephraim Wales Bull was buried. I had never heard of Ephraim Wales Bull, but the tour guide said he was the person who discovered the strand of Concord grapes. He never profited from the grapes because he died before they were marketed in jellies and jams.

The reason I share the story of Ephraim Wales Bull is because the epitaph on his gravestone reads, "He Sowed, Others Reaped."

I think that should be our mission … to keep sowing and allow others to reap.

Tony Pearce sowed; Jeff Walters reaped. Jeff sowed; I reaped. I sowed by writing this book, and now I hope you will reap from my Tuesday Morning Coaching and then sow for someone else.

The eight simple truths that Jeff shared helped me reboot my career and my life. I think the most important thing I learned was that success is not measured by the model car I drive, the size of my house or what title is on my business card. Success is much more than money and possessions.

I met and learned from successful people in occupations I had not paid much attention to before. I now describe a fire chief, coach, receptionist, golf pro, and cab driver as some of the most successful people I've known. I learned from each of them that success is achieved when we give the very best of what we have.

Every person I talked to on my journey, including Jeff, shared many common characteristics. They had a zest for life, adapted to challenges instead of running from them, built good relationships and brought out the best in those around them. Most importantly, though, each of them knows the difference between existing and living. They enjoy life to the fullest because they live life with a purpose – a clear sense of direction – and take positive actions daily that lead them closer to their purpose.

As for me, my career is back on track. Things are not perfect, but I'm able to deal with life's twists and turns more effectively. Our organization has adopted a No Matter What mentality, and we've enjoyed the freedom that comes when everyone accepts responsibility.

Our sales skyrocketed after we developed and implemented an And Then Some customer service strategy. And every Tuesday Morning, lessons from this book are being shared in every department. We have discovered, firsthand, that Knowledge Is Power.

My marriage is back on track, as well. I've continued to make dedicated time for Michele, and we are enjoying our lives together more than ever.

And, finally, my goals have changed – for the better. I've found the balance in all areas of my life as Jeff coached me to do. In fact, I recently turned down a promotion because it would have taken me away from accomplishing some of my personal and family goals. I feel like I am becoming a master goal-setter and goal-achiever.

Oh, and one more thing: After several golf lessons with David, I play to an eight handicap.

Yes, life is good. But the most important thing I learned from Jeff was the joy of sharing the simple truths of success – my gift to you.

Pass it on!

Tuesday Morning Wisdom
A Collection of Quotations

In times of stress and/or ambiguity, never make long-term,
life-changing decisions.

✦ ✦ ✦ ✦ ✦

Never in history has a situation improved on its own
while people sat there doing nothing.

✦ ✦ ✦ ✦ ✦

Some things you learn best while in the middle of a storm.

✦ ✦ ✦ ✦ ✦

Difficult always comes before easy.

✦ ✦ ✦ ✦ ✦

It is never a good idea to lie to yourself,
no matter how painful the truth may be.

✦ ✦ ✦ ✦ ✦

Successful people are not distracted by their success.
They are focused on mastering a combination of several
simple truths that – put together – create ongoing success.

✦ ✦ ✦ ✦ ✦

Keeping an open mind to different alternatives will expose
opportunities that you did not even know existed.

✦ ✦ ✦ ✦ ✦

Success is not about luck or the economy … it is about
making a conscious choice that No Matter What happens,
you will keep moving forward toward your goals.

✦ ✦ ✦ ✦ ✦

Most people are not committed enough
to make excellence an everyday event.

✦ ✦ ✦ ✦ ✦

Going the extra mile isn't that much harder than doing what
is required. In fact, it is often easier because there are not
many people traveling the extra mile ... so few in fact that
you may find yourself alone.

✦ ✦ ✦ ✦ ✦

People are searching for consistency –
where values do not change based on the situation of the day.

✦ ✦ ✦ ✦ ✦

When a person sacrifices his integrity,
nothing else really matters.

✦ ✦ ✦ ✦ ✦

It's rare that someone regrets giving it their all,
even if it doesn't work out.

✦ ✦ ✦ ✦ ✦

Complacency is the root of mediocrity, and mediocrity is
success's worst enemy – a far greater enemy, in fact, than failure.

✦ ✦ ✦ ✦ ✦

Never leave a problem ...
instead, move toward an opportunity.

✦ ✦ ✦ ✦ ✦

The true measure of success is being able to look in the
mirror and know that you had the courage to live the values
that are Above All Else in your life.

✦ ✦ ✦ ✦ ✦

It's okay to fail – everyone fails at some point –
but it's not okay to keep failing.

Growth and success are optional and if we choose that
option, we have to change.

✦ ✦ ✦ ✦ ✦

Most people who are unhappy in life are unhappy because
they don't have goals or a sense of purpose.

✦ ✦ ✦ ✦ ✦

Consciously attack procrastination by having the mindset that
there is no better time to get things done than right now.

✦ ✦ ✦ ✦ ✦

The most successful people consistently ask themselves,
"Is this the best use of my attention at this moment?"

✦ ✦ ✦ ✦ ✦

Multitask only if you want to do
multiple things poorly at once.

✦ ✦ ✦ ✦ ✦

Successful people make deliberate decisions
and conscious efforts directed toward a specific goal
they are trying to accomplish.

✦ ✦ ✦ ✦ ✦

The best way to increase knowledge is to teach someone else.

✦ ✦ ✦ ✦ ✦

You give more so that you will have more to give.

✦ ✦ ✦ ✦ ✦

The more you learn, the more you earn.

✦ ✦ ✦ ✦ ✦

Success is achieved when we give the very best of what we have.

Acknowledgements

Over the years, I have been blessed with some wonderful personal and professional coaches. My success has been molded and formed by those who took the time to listen and had the wisdom and willingness to share.

I am grateful for the people whose concepts generated ideas for lessons in this book. David Cook, the golf professional referenced in the book, taught me how to see it, feel it, and trust it. I recommend you read his book, *Golf's Sacred Journey*. The book will help your golf game but more importantly, it will improve your life. Thanks to Ralph Hendricks, who shared with me the intense training that firefighters endure in preparation for the unknown. And, thanks to my friend and pastor, Richard Jackson, who has taught me many of life's simple and everlasting truths.

I thank the CornerStone team: Alice Adams, Juli Baldwin, Barbara Bartlett, Ken Carnes, Lee Colan, Jim Garner, Kathleen Green, Kim Harris, Harry Hopkins, Michele Lucia, Suzanne McClelland, Melissa Monogue and our 24,000 customers who have remained loyal to CornerStone for the past 15 years. Please accept my deepest gratitude.

Without a doubt, I am one of the most fortunate people in the world. I thank God every day for allowing me the opportunity to live my dream.

To each person who reads this book, I hope that it will inspire you to your greatest success!

David Cottrell
Horseshoe Bay, TX

Nine ways to bring
Tuesday Morning Coaching
to life in your organization

Make the eight simple truths of success part of your team's daily business practices.

1. Keynote Presentation

Invite author David Cottrell to inspire your team to create greater success for your organization.

Contact Michele@DavidCottrell.com

2. Workshop

Facilitated by a certified CornerStone Leadership instructor, this 3- or 6-hour workshop reinforces the success principles from *Tuesday Morning Coaching*. Each participant will develop a personal action plan that can make an immediate and profound difference in their career and life.

Contact Michele@DavidCottrell.com.

3. One-on-One and Team Coaching

Certified, experienced coaches will coach you just as Jeff did Ryan in a series of sessions customized to your personal and/or organizational needs. You and your team will gain the support, insights, tools and accountability necessary to take your performance to the next level.

Contact Mitch@CornerStoneLeadership.com

4. Live Webinar

These 1½-hour live, Web-enabled sessions highlight key concepts and reinforce tools that will assist your organization. Your leaders will be able to learn from, interact with and ask questions of our subject-matter experts.

Contact Mitch@CornerStoneLeadership.com

5. PowerPoint™ Presentation

Enhance the *Tuesday Morning Coaching* experience in your organization with this professionally produced PowerPoint™ Slide Deck and easy-to-follow Facilitator's Guide. Use the presentation to kick off meetings and training sessions, or as a follow-up reinforcement tool. $99.95

Downloadable from www.CornerStoneLeadership.com

6. Online, Self-Paced Training Module

This interactive training experience reinforces the key concepts and principles of *Tuesday Morning Coaching*. Review critical lessons and complete a personal, printable action plan from the convenience of your home or office.

Visit www.CornerStoneLeadership.com

7. Audio CD

Listen and learn the eight simple truths of success during your commute, workout or anytime you need a boost. $19.95

www.CornerStoneLeadership.com or 888-789-5323

8. Coffee Mugs

Just like the gift from Ryan to Jeff. Reinforce the eight principles of success with your team every day.

Set of 4 – $39.95; Set of 24 – $199.95

www.CornerStoneLeadership.com
888-789-5323

9. Simple Truths Poster, Desktop Print & Pocket Card

Inspire your team and remind them daily of the Eight Simple Truths of Success with a striking poster, desktop print or laminated pocket card.

Poster: unframed – $19.95; framed – $89.95
Framed desktop print – $19.95
Set of 20 pocket cards – $19.95

www.CornerStoneLeadership.com or 888-789-5323

Recommended Resources for Additional Study

No Matter What!
> *Orchestrating Attitude: Getting the Best from Yourself and Others*

... And Then Some
> *You Gotta Get in the Game: How to Win in Business, Sales and Life*

Consider It Done
> *Sticking to It: The Art of Adherence*

Above All Else
> *Passionate Performance: Engaging Minds and Hearts to Conquer the Competition*

From Now On
> *The Eight Constants of Change: What Leaders Need to Know to Drive Change and Win*

See It, Feel It, Trust It, Do It!
> *Goal Setting for Results: Success Strategies for You and Your Organization*

Focus Inside Your Boat
> *TIME! 105 Ways to Get More Done Every Workday*

Knowledge Is Power
> *Monday Morning Choices ... 12 Powerful Ways to Go From Ordinary to Extraordinary*

Tuesday Morning Coaching **Package** –
all the books listed above plus
Tuesday Morning Coaching,
The Nature of Excellence perpetual calendar,
Monday Morning Motivation and
David Cottrell's Collection of Favorite Quotations ...
$129.95!
That's a savings of 25 percent!